ADVANCE PRAISE

The future is unknown, or is it? Mr. Setty takes a look into the future in 'Six Foot World' when many of us are currently stuck right here in present time and conditions. He explores the logical, predictable, and the possible and he does so from a East meets West mentality. This courageous view is calming, encouraging, and motivating, as even if it weren't to all roll-out as he theorizes, we could now make it so. Thank you, Rajesh for taking the time to wonder and support us all with a positive view out of the seeming abyss we're in. I'm on your side to help create our future.

—DAVID LEE JENSEN, Author, Speaker, Entrepreneur

When everyone is sheltering – physically and mentally – Raj is already helping us think about how the new world will look when we emerge after the Big Reset. Sadly no one, not even Raj, has all the answers. He admits his crystal ball is murky. But this book gives us some concepts, structures and approaches so that we can craft answers that will work for us and our communities. This is a powerful, compelling and uplifting read.

—IAN GOTTS, CEO : Speaker : Author : Bass Player

Especially relevant today, "Six Foot World" translates to and is applicable in all situations. Rajesh shares insightful views of how our lives and routines could be fundamentally transformed, in some cases beyond all recognition, post COVID-19. We all need to pay serious attention to the implications this has on all of us. However, it is not all bad news for us, thankfully. This book contains the tools and strategies we each can use to help us positively adapt and adjust beyond this initial crisis. A must read for everyone, period!

—IAN WOODLEY, Business Mentor and Transition Coach

It has been said that the definition of crazy is doing the same thing repeatedly and expecting different results. Today's world has changed in many dimensions. If we are to succeed, different ways to frame problems and opportunities are required. The old methods of achieving success may be of increasingly limited value. Rajesh points us in the right direction by giving us insightful and practical methods to break out of our outdated ways of seeing risk and reward. Timely, practical, and beneficial advice!

—DR. JEFFREY L. SAMPLER, Professor of Management Practice China Europe International Business School (CEIBS)

The game has changed and "Six Foot World" will keep your head above water in an epic storm of transformation. Clear thinking, concise insights, and leveraged strategies will enable you to expand your value as our ability to connect seems to contract. Grab this book now and be first in line to master this new game of life.

—KEN MCARTHUR, Filmmaker and Author of "The Impact Factor"

Rajesh provides a practical step by step approach to be successful in the post-COVID world.

—MR RANGASWAMI, Founder of Sandhill.com, Indiaspora and Eco-Forum

"Six Foot World" is a book that teaches the hygiene required for the mind during disruptive times. It's just not the view point of Rajesh Setty, he actually guides you to a point where you get the view of the future world.

—NAVEEN LAKKUR, Chief Innovation Coach at Institute of Inspiring Innovation

Rajesh is very generous to share his insights about the future (which are fantastic) but even more so are his suggestions about what could be done to gear ourselves up for the changes lurking around the corner, instead of getting a surprise jolt from it. Now, that is truly priceless.

The precious knowledge contained is definitely going to be useful in the post-COVID world. But there is much more packed in. This distilled mindset food is timeless. I literally consider it extremely pure gold and thus highly recommended reading for each and every entrepreneur, professional as well as an employee, who wishes to not just survive, but also to flourish in the new world we have stepped into. No wait, on second thoughts, I believe the phenomenal "Six Foot World" should actually be made mandatory reading, and that too, every few months!

—OMKAR NISAL, Head of Business Acquisitions at Neltronics.in

The maxim "change is the only constant in life" has been around for centuries, but at no time has it been more true than in the fast-paced and ever-changing world of today. In fact, we are in the midst of one of the most dramatic examples of global change ever. There is no going back, and we must adapt. Rajesh Setty is the voice of both sound reasoning and hope that we all need in this time of uncertainty. His love for humanity and emphasis on human connection is something I know personally, but will come through to all who read what he's written. He has put together this brilliant collection of his thoughts and ideas that will no doubt serve as a valuable resource to anyone who wants to get a head start on thriving, rather than merely surviving, in this new world that is upon us.

—RANA OLK, Professional Life and Neuro-Coach

The post-911 world vastly changed how we did air travel, in ways that no one had imagined. The post-COVID era is also going to be dramatically different in ways that we engage with one another – all of which we may not be able to yet fathom! Rajesh's book shines a light on many of the potential blind spots, providing a great set of implementable insights, changeable habits and practical tips. By embracing this wisdom, we can continue to engage in game-changing ways in the post-COVID world. Read this and respond gracefully or risk being reactive to the era that is being thrust upon all of us – whether you are ready or not!

—SATISH SHENOY, Technology Leader and Angel Investor

Our world is forever changed by COVID-19. Rajesh helps us start to grasp how things will be different in the coming years. His examples and "To Think" List ideas in each chapter help the reader start thinking about how their own life and business will change. An important book to help us understand how to adjust to our new environment starting today.

—STEVE SPONSELLER, Intellectual Property Attorney

SIX

FOOT

WORLD

RAJESH SETTY

SIX

HOW TO REIMAGINE THE

FOOT

FUTURE IN DISRUPTIVE TIMES

WORLD

IDEAPRESS
PUBLISHING

IDEAPRESS
PUBLISHING

Special Sales
Ideapress Books are available at a special discount for bulk purchases, for sales promotions and premiums, or for use in corporate training programs. Special editions, including personalized covers, a custom foreword, corporate imprints, and bonus content are also available.

To all the frontline people who lead the
fight against COVID-19 and save a few million lives while
putting their own lives at risk.

DISCLAIMER

I notice and observe things on topics that interest me and deduce patterns. I have strong opinions and points of view. I also admit that I have been wrong a few times before. So, treat this book as a point of view and not a prescription.

I have studied linguistic philosophy for years. I practice scheduled thinking times twice a week to process what's on my "To Think List." When the COVID-19 shelter-in-place was announced, I engaged in practicing "thinking time" every single day, after my daily meditation. This book was the result of what came out of those thinking times.

I am not a futurist, but everything I recommend in the book will help you even if things don't **exactly** pan out as outlined in my hypothesis. If they do, you are well prepared and if they don't, you are still way ahead.

CONTENTS

PART 1:
RESET IS NOT OPTIONAL

PART 2:
RE-AMPLIFY THE FUNDAMENTALS

PART 3.
REBOUND STARTER KIT

PART 4.
REFRAME AND CHARGE AHEAD

HOW TO MAKE THE MOST
OUT OF THIS BOOK

People around you have a huge influence on your outlook towards life. It goes without saying that you also have a similar influence on people around you.

Whether you are an entrepreneur, leader, or a teacher, you will benefit from people around you having a possibility mindset. This book has the potential to provide a lens of possibilities for your colleagues, employees, customers or your students, through which they can look at the world. Those few who read it will hopefully "infect" others with a gift of possibility thinking.

If you can bring people together, they can share their takeaways with each other. A few starter questions to answer in the future discussion:

1. What were your big takeaways from the book?
2. How are you going to apply one or two ideas from this book to your life and/or work?
3. How will you hold yourself accountable?

Sharing the answers to these questions as a group will surely benefit more than reading the book individually and pondering over your thoughts.

As you go through the concepts outlined in the following chapters, think of the contexts (be it your own or those from your network) where these concepts can be applied. This pause, reflect and think routine will help make the learning stick.

My wish for you is that this book will make you and those around you perceive the world as a place where problems shrink and possibilities expand.

FOREWORD

I have known Rajesh for several years now, so I was not surprised that he completed writing "**Six Foot World**" in record time.

This is probably the first business-esque book on the topic surrounding COVID-19. But, don't let the speed of execution color your judgement about the quality of the ideas in the book. Rajesh starts with a key takeaway right in the first chapter where he talks about the need to come up with a new label for what's happening with COVID-19 across the world. He follows with covering a few fundamentals to lay the necessary foundation to build upon future chapters where he shares ideas, strategies, tactics, and frameworks to think and act (rather than be shocked and withdrawn) to find and capitalize on possibilities that arise with this unprecedented change.

This book has several ideas and concepts that you wish you knew years ago. I am confident that you will have an edge in the marketplace if you read and act on even a few ideas in the book.

Rajesh practices what he preaches. Here is an example. The book has a heavy emphasis on reinvention and not surprisingly, Rajesh has done that within this book itself by creating something called **The Reader ROI Calculator**. You can determine the value you got out of the book by filling in a form.

If you are looking for value, halfway through the book, you will find that Rajesh has already over-delivered, but to make the most out of this book, you need to do your part – take a few of his insights to implementation as quickly as possible.

Dr. Mark Goulston
Author of "Just Listen" and other bestsellers
Los Angeles
April 2020

THIS TIME IT IS VERY DIFFERENT

[5-MINUTE READ]

Every time there is an event that shakes up the world, things change, sometimes temporarily and sometimes permanently.

If you don't believe me, read this.

Historian Nancy Bristow says that before the breakout of the 1918 Spanish Flu, it was a generally accepted practice to drink water out of a common cup in public places.

Well, that changed and the change was permanent.

Be it the Great Depression, a series of recessions, the Spanish Flu, the two world wars, or the market meltdown due to the mortgage crisis, things have changed.

In most cases, after a certain period of time, society came back to operating near normalcy. Of course, there was always change, but that was the change that comes with progress – heavily influenced by the technological shift and innovations.

In other words, the change was semi-elastic in nature during the crisis and returned to near normalcy post-crisis.

9/11 was different.

Unlike the changes brought about by the other events, this time it was permanent because it related to public security at large. The airport screenings seemed like an annoyance at first, but then it became a part of life. Nobody questioned it, because the rules had changed **for their own good.** Nobody wanted to take a chance and give an opening to terrorists who might cause more damage.

Under the hood, what really happened was that there was a breach of trust – a small segment of people with intentions to cause harm could show up anywhere, anytime. The unpredictable nature of their methods and actions caused uncertainty in the way we lived and worked. So, the changes imposed were accepted as normal.

Nicholas Nassim Taleb aptly named a category of such events as black swans: completely unimaginable before they occur, but easily explained post-occurrence.

And then, COVID-19 happened.

A choice was given. You either stay six feet apart or go six feet under.

Obviously, the world at large chose to stay six feet apart.

And, with that decision, in that very next instant, the world changed.

To identify potential stars⬚ raise the stakes. They will rise to the occasion when most others will run for the hills!

It's easy to describe it as **a black swan event** too. However, that would not fully describe COVID-19, as this time, the change is more different – the emphasis is on **more** here.

To distinguish between the change, first we have to see what makes this virus so different from any other viruses. The key is asymptomatic virality, which means that a carrier can transmit the virus to another person before the carrier notices any symptoms of the infection.

What does this mean?

Unlike the 9/11 scenario, where a small segment of people

with mal-intent were feared, here there is a breach of trust between people irrespective of their intent.

In other words, the unsaid social contract of **trustworthy-by-default** is downgraded to **suspect-by-default**.

This changes everything at a fundamental level on how we learn, grow, live, love, and work.

The magnitude of this change is unprecedented, but that can get masked by what labels you use to describe it.

If this had been a recession or a depression, you could have mentally painted a picture about the magnitude of the impact. Well, you probably know that this is more complex than those scenarios.

You could call this as a black swan event – an unprecedented event when it happens, but a very explainable post event.

The term "black swan" still does not do justice to what is happening.

Unless we find the right label for this phenomenon, we will be at a disadvantage because we will diagnose the problem wrong, mis-calculate the impact and hence will not take the necessary actions with the right speed and intensity.

Imagine you have a fever and you take your body temperature. It shows 105-degrees, but for some reason, you read it as 99-degrees. That error will wreak havoc because as mentioned before, you diagnosed the problem wrong, you will mis-calculate the impact and then fail to take the necessary actions with speed and intensity to solve the problem.

I suggest that we call this a **black bevy** event.

Bevy is the term for a group of swans. Black bevy in essence would have an impact of simultaneous occurrence of multiple black swan events across the world. It is an event that is unimaginable before it happens, but easily explainable post the event. More importantly, it changes the way we live in a significant way.

In recent history, I can't think of a "black bevy" scale event. In a geographical setting, India faced something like this when the Government implemented a demonetization policy. It was not a health crisis, but an economic one and that lasted for a brief period when things started to settle into an equilibrium of the new normal.

The "black bevy" kind of events will be gripping reading material for those in the future who will study what happened today in their history class. But, it's not going to be easy for most of us who are living here now witnessing the events unfolding right in front of our eyes.

They are already calling the children born during this period as "Generation C." I won't be surprised if BC would take on a new meaning: Before COVID.

Rachel Voyles, who runs Colorado Movement Therapy, captured the essence of the problem this can create brilliantly in her message below:

One of the things I tell clients and friends is that long, slow hugs are one of the best things you can do for stress management.

Long hugs also release oxytocin, reduce heart rate and

blood pressure... plus all the just obvious psychological benefits of getting a purposeful moment of love amidst a world that has a hard time slowing down.

Here is the preview of upcoming attractions. On March 25, 2020, American Airlines sent this message with the changes (temporarily, they say) they have made in response to the COVID-19 threat:

Hello Rajesh,

American has temporarily changed a number of policies in response to COVID-19. These changes include a relaxed seating policy, reduced food and beverage service, and suspension of checked pets.

We've relaxed our seating policy to enable customers to practice social distancing on board whenever possible.

For the safety of our customers and flight attendants, we're temporarily suspending food and beverage service on flights under 2,200 miles (typically less than 4½ hours). Limited beverages will be available upon request. On flights over 2,200 miles (typically longer than 4½ hours), we will continue to offer a streamlined food and beverage service.

Because schedule changes increase the risk of leaving a pet stranded, all checked pet service will be suspended beginning March 25. Carry-on pets and emotional service animals are still allowed.

All details regarding these temporary modifications can be found on aa.com. We appreciate your trust in us in these uncertain times, and we'll continue working to keep you safe.

A couple of months later in early May, 24 Hour Fitness (a fitness chain in the US) sent a short video to all its members about how they are making changes internally to resume service. Here are some highlights from that video:

- 24 Hour Fitness centers will no longer operate at night (Yes, all of us can see the irony in the company name. I'm sure the 24 Hour Fitness executives know it too, but they have to do what they have to do in the short-term. They need an adaptable business model to match the new reality.)
- You will need to book your workout times via their app.
- After every workout session, the gym will close for 30 minutes to sanitize all the equipment.
- Classes will have fewer people in the group so that everyone can maintain social distancing.

There is more. But you've got the idea. Companies around you are adapting, and those who want to maintain the status quo just bought a ticket to mediocrity at best.

Welcome to the new world of **Minimum Viable Touch (MVT)**.

Let the games begin.

ONE KEY TAKEAWAY
FROM THIS SECTION:

CHOOSE THE AREA OF IMPACT:	☐ PERSONAL ☐ PROFESSIONAL ☐ BUSINESS

THE TAKEAWAY:

Pause, Reflect and Record: Go to Appendix I (The Reader ROI Calculator) and fill in the details for this section.

PART 1

RESET
IS NOT
OPTIONAL

You have been invited to the meeting to reset the world.
Attendance is mandatory. Ready or not, here comes the reset.

IT'S NOT THE RULES, IT'S THE GAME

[3-MINUTE READ]

Imagine this situation.

You are playing a game of chess. You're forced to stop it when you're half-way through and you are told that you can resume the play the next day.

But, the next morning, there is a surprise waiting for you. Instead of a chess board, there is a Go game board.

You frantically try to figure out where your chess game has been moved to until someone tells you, "We are no longer playing chess. You are welcome to join the Go game."

"But, I don't even know what this game is. I want to continue playing chess," you protest.

All in vain though because you are told, "Playing the earlier game is no longer an option. Either you can play the game of Go or you can move to the sidelines and let others play."

You cannot believe it.

You feel that this is not fair.

It's not the rules that have changed, but the game itself. Your mastery of rules, strategies, and tactics in the earlier game is suddenly relegated to near-irrelevance.

It's not the **rules** that have changed, but the game itself. Your mastery of the rules, strategies & tactics of the earlier game has been relegated to near-irrelevance

1|62

You don't like this, but it seems like nobody cares about what you like or dislike.

If this appears like a bad dream for you, you are in for a rude awakening.

This is metaphorically what will be happening with the world as a result of the COVID-19 black bevy event.

Here is the sequence:

THE PRE-COVID ERA

You are busy with your life and work, dealing with the usual challenges in your personal and professional lives.

DURING THE COVID SEASON

You are busy keeping yourself and your family safe and get whatever work you can get done.

THE POST-COVID ERA

You resume your life, assuming that you can pick up where you left off. But, here is where you are in for a surprise. You realize that everything has changed. Yes, everything.

The genesis of the shock is at the level of fundamental assumptions and worldviews that had upgraded themselves to the level of "truths" you didn't have to revisit until this point in time.

Why? Because these assumptions and worldviews are at the core of how we learn, grow, love, live, work, and play. This is the way you grew up. This is what everyone around you thought and for all practical purposes, this is (was) your "truth".

But, not anymore.

WHAT'S NOT CHANGED...

While you don't have a choice but to play a different game, what has not changed is the need to play a long game. I often say that a shortcut is the longest route to a meaningful destination.

LONG ✓
WRONG ✗

PLAYING THE VERY LONG GAME IS YOUR INSURANCE AGAINST PLAYING A VERY WRONG GAME !

SOURCE: WWW.NAPKINSIGHTS.COM/NAPKIN/849/

Now, let's just look at a few implications of the latest buzzword, social distancing in the next chapter.

SUGGESTIONS FOR YOUR "TO THINK" LIST

1. What is one thing I should stop doing that would help me be more effective?

2. What is one thing I should start doing that would help me be more effective?

_____

_____

_____

_____

_____

_____

_____

_____

_____

_____

_____

_____

_____

_____

_____

_____

_____

_____

_____

_____

ONE KEY TAKEAWAY
FROM THIS SECTION:

CHOOSE THE AREA OF IMPACT:	☐ PERSONAL ☐ PROFESSIONAL ☐ BUSINESS

THE TAKEAWAY:

Pause, Reflect and Record: Go to Appendix I (The Reader ROI Calculator) and fill in the details for this section.

TO TOUCH OR NOT TO TOUCH IS THE QUESTION, LITERALLY AND FIGURATIVELY

[4-MINUTE READ]

Social distancing was the right thing to do to break the chain because of the asymptomatic virality of the COVID-19 virus.

You never know who is a carrier, so why take a chance?

Even when the situation comes back to near normalcy and the COVID-19 becomes history, the long-term damage done by the "the reason for social distancing" is near-irreversible for the foreseeable future.

Before COVID-19, the question that would run in your mind when you met a friend used to be:

"Should I give them a hug or not?"

Now the question is: "Should I touch them or keep my distance?"

In the middle of the COVID-19 season, at one end was self-quarantine and at the other, maintaining a distance of at least six feet. No handshakes.

What would be a few implications of just this one behavior change?

At the outset, it looks like we can replace the handshake by a fist bump, a bow, a high-five, a toe bump, an elbow bump or the traditional Namaste from the East.

That would be trivializing and diluting the problem.

Here are a few areas where you could see an impact (in no particular order).

Businesses which run on crowds will be completely reinvented. A few examples are conferences, sporting events, music festivals, trade shows, company gatherings, large-scale, in-person training programs, and large religious gatherings to name a few.

This seems like the first order problem.

The second order derivatives of this problem is how it will impact the entire ecosystem and the cottage industry that is dependent on the events industry. Let's double-click on that and see who it affects:

- Hotels that host these events and the attendees
- Event organizers who put these events together
- Catering services that supply food for these events
- Speakers who make money through keynotes and other speeches
- Sound system providers for the events
- Videographers and photographers for the events
- Travel to and fro to the city where the event is happening and within the city
- Travel agents who manage travel for executives who are attending the events
- Restaurants around the location of the events
- Mom and pop shops that serve the needs of travelers
- Travel-related goods starting with travel gear to grooming kits
- Businesses that pay lots of money to operate stores in airports, hoping for foot traffic
- Travel insurance companies
- Airport car rentals
- Books and magazines that used to get a boost during travel
- Hotel entertainment networks
- Software and hardware providers that help manage the events smoothly
- Entertainers and artists that depend on performing at these events
- Tourist hotspots around the city where events are happening
- House sharing services such as AirBnB

This is just the tip of the iceberg. There are hundreds of other businesses that will get impacted just from this one human behavior change.

The above list is just an example to show the vicious downward spiral of things to come. If you are not in any of the above businesses, it would be naive to assume that the after-effects won't impact you. Everyone on this planet will be affected either directly or indirectly.

It is not if, but when your turn will come to pay the price in some way.

NOT TOUCHING ANYTHING NEW

My friend recently joked that he still gets half a dozen emails about clothing items while the entire state had been under lockdown for a few weeks already. He said, "Raj, what am I going to do with all the new clothes they want me to buy? I've been in my pajamas and t-shirts for the last few weeks!"

This slump in shopping can easily extend to other related areas.

I was in a group discussion in one of the masterminds I belong to. A small business entrepreneur was sharing that her entire pipeline for the next six months vanished within a couple of weeks. She is in the wedding business. A total of 15 weddings were either cancelled or postponed and the new dates were yet to be set.

Then the negative impact continues with select stores closing, needing less supply, affecting the factories down the chain.

So, in summary, more people will prefer to not touch anything new.

Well, what could you do?

About "more people not touching anything new", pretty much nothing.

However, on "what you can do next", here is where you could begin:

First, there is a real need to stop, reflect, and take an inventory of all your current skills and talents that you deployed to create meaningful value in the past.

Second, honestly assess which of those skills and talents can continue to be deployed to create value in the post-COVID world.

Third, after that gap analysis, think about what new skills you need to acquire rapidly so that you can continue to create meaningful value.

Fourth, reinvent to get ready.

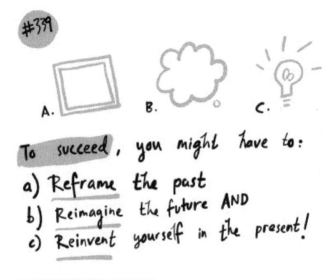

#339

A.   B.   C.

To **succeed**, you might have to:

a) Reframe the past
b) Reimagine the future AND
c) Reinvent yourself in the present!

SOURCE: WWW.NAPKINSIGHTS.COM/NAPKIN/339

SUGGESTIONS FOR YOUR "TO THINK" LIST

1. What are the second order effects on my work because of the effects of COVID (and people not being able to meet as usual)?

_____

_____

_____

_____

_____

_____

_____

ONE KEY TAKEAWAY
FROM THIS SECTION:

**CHOOSE THE
AREA OF IMPACT:**

☐ PERSONAL
☐ PROFESSIONAL
☐ BUSINESS

THE TAKEAWAY:

Pause, Reflect and Record: Go to Appendix I (The Reader ROI Calculator) and fill in the details for this section.

RADICAL REINVENTION IS NOT A LUXURY, BUT A NECESSITY

[4-MINUTE READ]

Your worldviews, strategies, and tactics that used to make things happen will most probably stop working effectively, in the post-COVID world.

So, a replay of the above is out of the question.

What is necessary and urgent is reinvention.

What does that mean?

Let's say you did not exist here. Imagine you were dropped on this planet one day after the COVID crisis dies down.

After a few days of observing everything around you, you will determine what skills you need to thrive in this world. Imagine you acquired all the necessary skills and became the person you and those around you would be proud of.

The path to becoming that person is how you reinvent yourself.

Radical reinvention is not a luxury, but a necessity because how the world operates has changed. So, incremental improvements in what you bring to the table are meaningless. Radical reinvention forces you to look at all your aspects and your work end-to-end and not restrict it to fixing something that seems to be broken.

How radical should the reinvention be?

Well, you are the only person who can decide that. My suggestion is to be prepared and welcome whatever degree of radicalness that is required to make it happen.

An analogy would be a full-body check up with a DNA analysis from the company 23AndMe to review your overall health and a plan of action from a doctor and a nutritionist.

The world is looking for a different offer from you and not a better-than-before version of what you are already bringing.

It is important to note that reinventing yourself is not going to give you an upgrade. Rather, think of it like this. Without reinventing yourself, you won't have an entry ticket to the new game. You will be relegated to the sidelines where all you can do is watch others play.

Now, let us talk about one key challenge and one progress marker for this initiative.

The key challenge that you will face is the reluctance to change and the willingness to unlearn. You don't need a primer about the need for these two inter-related items. Without the willingness to unlearn, the canvas is too crowded for you to add something new. Without the willingness to change, you will go back to what you were doing before, resulting in a common phenomenon called "going in circles."

It is outside the scope of this book to cover both of them, but there is enough written about how to unlearn and navigate change with grace.

Now, coming to the progress marker. You need a progress marker to check on yourself to ensure that you are actually moving the needle in real life and not manufacturing progress in your head.

> "The electric light did not come from the
> continuous improvement of candles."
> **—OREN HARARI**

If you truly reinvent yourself, you will shift the criteria with which the marketplace puts a value for your offer. You will stand out with ease.

Let me give you a couple of examples that all of us are very familiar with:

First, iPod from Apple:

When Apple created the iPod, they did not create something that is marginally better than the other CD players.

In fact, you could not compare the iPod to a CD player. It was a different offering compared to what existed in the marketplace. Result: 375,000 units of iPod were sold in the first year. The iPod set the standard for how music was consumed by the world.

Second, Kindle from Amazon:

Amazon did not create another eBook reader. They created a platform with which readers could interact with digital content. Amazon worked with partners that include major publishers to enable one-click access to digital content. Result: 500,000 units of Amazon Kindle were sold in the first year. Kindle set the standard for how to distribute digital content.

If you observe both the examples above, you will see that both offerings shifted the criteria for how they should be compared with existing offerings in the marketplace. They were not "also-ran"s that were marginally better than the existing offerings. They were truly different ones.

On one level, we are all unique and on another level, we are all common. If your offer to the world is common, you are competing with a boatload of people.

Why?

Simply because everything that's common responds with a similar answer for the criteria set to measure it. If you are a part of the common, the only answer you have is to work hard and provide a better answer. When others respond with a similar strategy, there is a dog fight and everyone in the game is in trouble.

A better way to solve this dilemma is to be that someone who gets measured by criteria that are different from the current market standards. That is precisely where you will bring out your uniqueness and more.

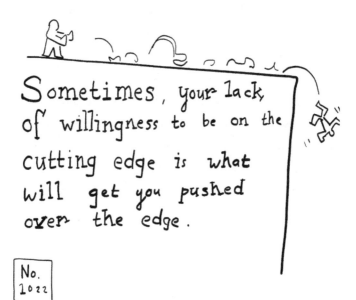

Sometimes, your lack of willingness to be on the cutting edge is what will get you pushed over the edge.

No. 1022

SOURCE: WWW.NAPKINSIGHTS.COM/NAPKIN/1022/

You can fall into the common trap and try to match the current offerings. In that case, you will need to offer everything that fits the standard criteria set by the marketplace and a lot more. There's another option. Offer something that will make the existing offers in the marketplace seem irrelevant. In simple terms, you need to sufficiently distinguish yourself in the marketplace to make your mark and demand a premium.

The key questions to ask yourself are:

- For how long more will the underlying need that I am serving and getting paid for continue to be relevant?
- What new needs will emerge that are meaningful enough that the marketplace is willing to pay someone?
- What steps should I take now so that I am the right person for that opportunity to serve?
- What relationships should I invest in so that I can be at the right place to be considered for that opportunity?
- Who can help me (even if I have to pay them) to accelerate my journey to the right place?
- How do I know that I am on the right path?
- How will I hold myself accountable to see through this change?

SUGGESTIONS FOR YOUR "TO THINK" LIST

What are the biggest barriers that my current and potential clients have for working with me in the current situation?

_____

_____

_____

_____

_____

_____

_____

_____

_____

_____

_____

_____

_____

_____

_____

_____

_____

_____

_____

ONE KEY TAKEAWAY
FROM THIS SECTION:

CHOOSE THE AREA OF IMPACT:	☐ PERSONAL ☐ PROFESSIONAL ☐ BUSINESS

THE TAKEAWAY:

Pause, Reflect and Record: Go to Appendix I (The Reader ROI Calculator) and fill in the details for this section.

NOT HIGHER INTENSITY, BUT GREATER RE-IMAGINATION

[4-MINUTE READ]

If you look around, you will see that everyone around you is stressed out like never before. Most of them will also be working way harder than ever before.

Just by sheer social pressure, you feel like you too are overwhelmed and you too want to crank up the intensity. In most other scenarios, cranking up the intensity will yield results fast!

Not here.

What you need is greater reimagination.

Let us dig a bit deeper into this.

If repeating what you were doing earlier yields results now, then reinvention and re-imagination will no longer be necessary. What you were doing earlier was taking you in the wrong direction. Cranking up the intensity on the previous work will continue to take you in the wrong direction – only faster.

There is a need for greater reimagination here because we have entered uncharted territory where everything has to be figured out. There is no history being repeated so there is nothing to draw from our experience.

Here is why greater re-imagination is difficult to practice. It's a phenomenon I call **a double-blindspot.**

The first blindspot:

When you increase your intensity on whatever you were doing, you will see a small positive uptick, making you think that you might have the right strategy. So, you crank up the intensity even more, leading to a bit more positive uptick. There is a ray of hope for you although you are feeling a bit tired. But, you are committed, so you keep going, cranking up the intensity even more.

So, what happens next is...

Nothing.

Everyone has a breaking point and you have it too.

You give up and resort to what everyone around you is doing. Blame the circumstances, the government, or just luck.

SOURCE: WWW.NAPKINSIGHTS.COM/NAPKIN/811

You try to reimagine what's next. Since it's not magic to manifest what you imagine, you don't get any feedback on it immediately. You work on making it a reality, but not with your full heart and soul.

After a while, you think what you reimagined is flawed and you do the exercise again.

The result:

The same: Nothing.

You give up and resort to what everyone around you is doing. Blame the circumstances, the government, or just luck.

This is one of those areas where you can put your ego aside and get help from a trusted mentor to guide you through the process. You will save time, energy and avoid a lot of frustration.

Naveen Lakkur, author of the book 'a Little Extra', says "... re-imagination could make companies relevant with a possibility of extraordinary results". Companies need to innovate, else they die. He strongly believes that innovation is that positive change which everyone is capable of exercising. He defines innovation in simple terms as (a) making something better, (b) doing something different and (c) creating something new.

He also explains it with a couple of examples:

1. Imagine a company, which manufactures women's inner garments. Irrespective of which location in the world they would be in, there is a high chance that their company would be temporarily shut down. If they are willing to go a little extra, they can re-imagine each brassiere as two masks. They already have the required raw material, technology know-how, and suitability of the existing design with the cups having proven the test of time as skin-friendly, and comfortable. If only they are willing to go a little extra and do something different, they can stay relevant during the COVID-19 crisis and will get the required permission to change the status of their product as essential, enabling them to shift from a lockdown state to a log-in state. Anyway, masks are not going to go out of style for the near future. It might even become the new style or even lifestyle.

2.   Let's consider a sports equipment company. Sure, sports events are suspended. But re-imagine their popular full face headgear and the poncho (trek gear) coming together to create something new which would become a PPE (Personal Protective Equipment) gear. Both the head gear and poncho have been tested for hard conditions and they have performed well. Are you now already imagining how a sports company can become relevant and play a new game of impact?

We also have Elon Musk as a poster-child of re-imagionation. He re-imagined Tesla, a car manufacturing company, to build medical ventilators during this crisi. Tesla dared to disrupt their own business model. By repurposing the majority of the auto parts and components to manufacture ventilators, their innovation made them relevant and created a possibility to contribute meaningfully during these disruptive times.

Re-imagine and increase the odds of winning.

SUGGESTIONS FOR YOUR "TO THINK" LIST

1. How can I turn my client's top barrier in working with me into a question?

Example:

Top Barrier: We can't visit our prospects.

Turned into a question: How can we get started even if we can't visit our prospects?

_____

_____

_____

_____

_____

_____

_____

_____

_____

_____

_____

_____

_____

_____

_____

_____

_____

_____

ONE KEY TAKEAWAY
FROM THIS SECTION:

CHOOSE THE AREA OF IMPACT:

☐ PERSONAL
☐ PROFESSIONAL
☐ BUSINESS

THE TAKEAWAY:

Pause, Reflect and Record: Go to Appendix I (The Reader ROI Calculator) and fill in the details for this section.

9 UNCOMMON REASONS FOR THE RISE OF STRESS

[4-MINUTE READ]

COVID-19 can be termed as an "equal opportunity peace-of-mind destroyer." This virus has probably created more "riches to rags" stories in the history of mankind. Not just that, COVID-19 has influenced changing the societal operating system of this world immediately making several programs that were running on the previous societal operating system become redundant.

This is what is creating the new reality. This changing world creates many reasons for the rise of stress. Here are nine of them:

1. LIMITLESS POSSIBILITIES, UNLIMITED COMPETITION

Thomas Friedman wrote a book titled "The World is Flat" years ago and the emphasis there was globalization. It was a wonderful book that had a great title and there were areas where the world seemed to be flat, but mostly it was not. COVID-19 in a matter of months pushed the world to become more flat than ever before.

On one end of the COVID influence, there are unlimited possibilities. You will read more about why in the chapter "Capitalize on the fundamental reframe" later in the book. On the other end of this has unlimited competition. It cuts both ways.

Your playground to make a difference is the entire globe. Unfortunately, your competition is coming from the entire globe.

In a flat world, You can no longer rest on your laurels of being a "local hero" because there is rarely something that's "local."

What can you do: Invest in yourself as if there is no tomorrow.

2. ALWAYS ON; MOSTLY OFF

Look around. Do you see people glued to their smartphones? They are the lifetime members of the "always on" club.

What about you?

Always on is not a bad club to belong to if you know how to take advantage of it. In reality, being "always on" to something somewhere else will result in you being "mostly off" to the here and present.

You can be guaranteed that any kind of learning and growth will be absent when you are not fully present.

What can you do: Start a meditation practice. It will not only help you become present, it will also ground you. Here are some practices that have helped me (in no particular order):

a)   Inner Engineering by Sadhguru Jaggi Vasudev

b)   Happiness Program by Sri Sri Ravishankar

c)   Higher, Deeper and Beyond (HDB) by Mahatria

3. ENGAGED EVERYWHERE; FOCUSED NOWHERE

You are engaged everywhere because information is coming from you from all directions. Result: You will most certainly be focused nowhere.

You might say that in the new world we are permanently living in a state of continuous partial attention to everything.

If that's the case, how is it working for you?

In the words of Seth Godin, if you are NOT "shipping" something meaningful in a reasonable timeframe, it is time to re-look at everything - especially the "need to focus" part.

What can you do: Try anything that will put you in the "focus" mode even for short bursts of time. You can start with a technique like Promodoro technique.

4. YOU CAN SEDUCE THROUGH STORYTELLING; YOU CAN BE SEDUCED THROUGH STORYTELLING

Stories sell. You can tell compelling stories to sell a lot of things. That's a good thing.

If you are not guarded, you may not realize that thousands of companies are using compelling stories to seduce you to buy their stuff - or at least make you think that whatever they are selling is something you badly NEED. A lot of things in life are "nice to have", but good storytelling will upgrade the "nice to have" to "must have now" status.

The problem?

Unchecked, the growing list of "must have" things is a surefire way to stress and frustration.

What can you do: Invest in learning the art and craft of storytelling. You will reap rewards for the rest of your life.

5. THE SURFACE IS SHINY; THE FOUNDATION IS SHAKY

A lot of techniques and tactics are at the surface level. The surface is usually shiny. If you get attracted to the surface level techniques and tactics and think that you are making investment in yourself, you are mistaken.

Growth happens when your foundation gets stronger. Too

much focus on the surface will leave your foundation shaky the result of which is that your progress is temporary.

What do you do: You can get by with surface-level skills for quite some time, but in the long run, only depth will help you win. Pick one or two areas that you love and make it a daily practice to invest more in getting better at thes skils

6. FUN; NO FUN

While you are trying to make meaning in your life, if you are like most people, you can't resist the temptation to check what's happening in the social networks.

When you do, you will notice that there is so much fun happening in everyone's life.

Someone just got married

A few people were on vacation.

A lot of people went to fancy restaurants.

A few people were celebrating some life events - birthdays, anniversaries, graduations etc.

A lot of people were sharing how cool their kids were.

Overall, there is no dearth of fun in the social networks. They had plenty of it.

What about your life? It's a different story. You are swamped with work and no time to breathe. Looks like there is fun in abundance everywhere. Can't seem to find it anywhere in your life.

Right?

Wrong.

The nature of social networks is that people publish their select moments in their life and amplify them. Their select moments should rarely be compared to your "non-select" moments.

What can you do: Regularly take social media holidays. You will see your productivity soar instantly. We think we are using social media products and we need to be reminded that WE are the products for social media.

7. EXPERT TODAY; DATED TOMORROW

Gone are the days where you invest in yourself for a few years and reap the rewards of the same for the rest of your life. Whether you want it or not, real school starts when you finish your academic schooling.

You can pay the price to learn or you pay the price for not paying the price to learn. Your choice. Your expert status on anything is short-lived. If you don't have the mindset of a lifelong learner, you will be dated sooner rather than later.

What can you do: Learn to read the world, or follow people who have been doing this for a while.

8. RIGHT CONTENT; WRONG CONTEXT

Warning. This is a trap.

Suppose, let's say you want to be a lifelong learner and start reading expert advice (including reading this book) please remember that no author can create content that will specifically resonate with your exact present context.

It is YOUR responsibility to take that content, fine tune it for your context, test it out and then apply the lessons for good if the tests succeed.

Even the right content works only in the right context.

What can you do: Later in the book, there is a chapter on instituting a "no insight left behind" policy. Make a note to incorporate the practice outlined there.

9. UNLIMITED CONTENT; LIMITED TIME

There is no problem with the availability of all kinds of content. In fact, the problem is the other way around. There is too much content. There is not enough time to consume all that good content that's out there.

Thoughtful curation is key.

You are smart and ambitious. But, you are busy as hell. You have to find your own path to access learning tools that are designed to fit your lifestyle. Otherwise, you will experience a FOMO-induced stress

What can you do: Look for highly curated knowledge and advice sources rather than have a high signal-to-noise ratio. One such source for sound advice is our own app Audvisor (more about that at the end of the book).

SUGGESTIONS FOR YOUR
"TO THINK" LIST

Reflect on what are the "real factors' that are causing you stress and what you can do to address them with resources that you already have.

_____

_____

_____

_____

_____

_____

_____

_____

_____

_____

_____

_____

_____

_____

_____

_____

_____

_____

_____

ONE KEY TAKEAWAY
FROM THIS SECTION:

**CHOOSE THE
AREA OF IMPACT:**

☐ PERSONAL
☐ PROFESSIONAL
☐ BUSINESS

THE TAKEAWAY:

Pause, Reflect and Record: Go to Appendix I (The Reader
ROI Calculator) and fill in the details for this section.

PART 2

RE-AMPLIFY THE FUNDAME-NTALS

Some fundamental concepts are timeless. In our busy lives, sometimes we forget to revisit and strengthen the knowledge of these fundamentals. In this section, I will cover a few concepts that are fundamental, yet very important in the new reality.

Note that as you read some of the chapters in this section, you might be tempted to find a direct connection to what's happening now in the world. Let me save you the trouble. There is no direct connection. But, mastering these fundamentals will give you an edge over others who are just looking for shortcuts.

RETHINK THE FUNDAMENTAL QUESTION

[2-MINUTE READ]

In times of crisis, how you show up makes a big difference. The "how you show up" is heavily influenced by the fundamental question.

You may ask yourself, "How can I find the next opportunity?"

This is a good question, but unfortunately, not a powerful one.

When you are in the eye of the storm, everyone around you seems to ask the same question, creating a sort of a rat race.

You can tweak the question a little bit to make it more powerful.

And that version might look like this:

"How can I become an opportunity for someone else?"

NATURAL QUESTION:

HOW CAN I FIND THE NEXT ~~OPPORTUNITY~~?

UPGRADED QUESTION:

HOW CAN I BECOME AN ~~OPPORTUNITY~~ FOR SOMEONE ELSE?

1165.

Let's take a case in point.

Times are tough and you are trying to find a new job. That's the context. Now, let's go over the two options above and you will see the difference instantly.

Option 1: How can you find your next opportunity?

A new job, no doubt, will be an opportunity for you. But that's a one-sided perspective. If you want to create a real opportunity, you need to create a compelling offer for your prospective employer.

Do they see you as another person scrambling for a seat?

If so, then you've been defined as someone who wants to take something scarce (employment) from them.

Option 2: How can you be an opportunity for someone else?

Do they see you as someone who offers them opportunities?

Will your presence in the job create new opportunities, expand possibilities, or solve a current headache that keeps them up at night?

If so, you're giving more value than they are asking for.

The bottom line is that there are enough opportunities for you out there if you can be the opportunity for enough people.

By now, you would have noticed the key difference between the two questions.

a) How can I find my next opportunity?

b) How can I be an opportunity for someone else?

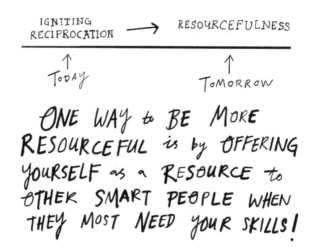

ONE WAY to BE MORE RESOURCEFUL is by OFFERING YOURSELF as a RESOURCE to OTHER SMART PEOPLE WHEN THEY MOST NEED YOUR SKILLS!

No.
1002

SOURCE: WWW.NAPKINSIGHTS.COM/NAPKIN/1002/

The latter one puts you in the mood of serving and the former question puts you in the mood of self-serving. The latter will deposit into your karma account and the former will withdraw from the same account.

This is the difference that makes all the difference in the world.

ONE KEY TAKEAWAY
FROM THIS SECTION:

**CHOOSE THE
AREA OF IMPACT:**

☐ PERSONAL
☐ PROFESSIONAL
☐ BUSINESS

THE TAKEAWAY:

Pause, Reflect and Record: Go to Appendix I (The Reader ROI Calculator) and fill in the details for this section.

CAPITALIZE ON TO-THINK LISTS

[5-MINUTE READ]

Nobody questions the value of practicing deep thinking. The problem is not with knowing, it is usually in doing. If deep thinking was important during ordinary times, it is extremely important in disruptive times.

But...

The news and sensationalist cycles running around us has an impact on us. They make us practice surface-level thinking as they shift our attention from one drama to another. The drama is everywhere – in newspapers, news portals, blogs, social platforms, WhatsApp groups and even in your text messages. When a crisis like the COVID-19 hits, everybody around us is reacting rather than responding.

It seems like the whole world wants you to react.

But, what's needed is the exact opposite of all of this –a response as a result of deep thinking. A practice of creating and processing to-think lists will help you get there.

Here we go.

Before we dive deep into the concept of "to think lists", we need to revisit the more common practice of creating and processing "to do lists." You will see that by the end of this discussion, we would have made a case for "To Think Lists".

So, the cycle goes something like this:

1. Make a to-do list.

2. Start checking off things in the list.

3. Rearrange spillover to-do items for a future date (of course throw away a few)

4. Go back to step 1 the next day.

Here are some things you need to think about when you create your to-do lists:

1. What gets into the to-do list?

2. Why do they get into the to-do list?

3. What do you like and don't like about what gets into the to-do list?

4. How fast is the to-do list getting cleared?

5. What is your feeling when things get cleared or remain undone in the to-do list?

The biggest influencer that will make this effective is **your quality of thinking.**

Only **you** can work on improving your quality of thinking.

Your quality of thinking definitely influences the actions you take, but that is not easily visible to others. The results matter to the stakeholders, the process and effort to get those results - not so much.

For instance, if you produce a report in the promised seven days, the client is happy. They won't care whether you spent 140 hours in those seven days, or whether you were able to get this done by spending five hours a day. The "how" and the "how much effort was involved" may not be important for the client, but it should be very important for you. See in the former case, you pretty much killed yourself and in the latter case you probably got this done like it was a walk in the park.

What made the difference?

Your quality of thinking.

Incorporating the practice of "to think lists" is probably the fastest way to improve your quality of thinking.

A TO-THINK LIST

Most of your education was all about doing well. Your curriculum didn't include even a few topics on how to think well. It was left for you to figure that out. You may not be a college-going student, but you can still make a change with this habit.

A to-think list contains things that you want (need) to think about.

I use a to-think list like how I use a to-do list. I put on it what I have to think about in the future. When I set aside time for myself, I have a handy list of things to think about.

983

GUARANTEE

If you ARE LOOKING to START SOMETHING SIGNIFICANT **AFTER** you HAVE EVERYTHING you NEED, THE **ONLY** THING your PLAN GUARANTEES is THAT you WILL KEEP LOOKING!

SOURCE: WWW.NAPKINSIGHTS.COM/NAPKIN/983/

I keep adding things that I want to think about to my to-think list. Every week, I set aside about two blocks of 90 minutes of machine-free time to think about what is on the to-think list. There is only a pen, some paper and myself during this time.

In the last decade, every big thing that I have achieved has been influenced and amplified by practicing thinking times based on a to-think list.

SUMMARY

If to-do lists can improve your productivity directly, to-think lists can improve your quality of thinking (and hence improve your productivity, indirectly).

Note: Whatever you are reading now is the result of weeks of disciplined thinking as I processed the one item on my to-think list: COVID-19.

BONUS: THE LET-GO LIST

Here is a bonus list that you should consider maintaining – the let-go list, which has things that you should stop doing. If you want to get fancy, you can also call it a not-to-do list.

Here are a few items to serve as examples to put in there. You can add/modify/delete from this list to make it your own.

1. The feeling of entitlement
2. Chasing something that's too good to be true
3. Lack of accountability
4. Too much focus on the short-term
5. Too much focus on the long-term
6. Expertise in generating excuses for lack of results
7. Undeserved credit
8. Holding back on genuine appreciation
9. Expecting something for FREE
10. Not giving your best for FREE

The reason to maintain and work on such a list is to reduce noise in your head, increase your effectiveness, and clear up clutter to make way for capacity expansion to do more important things.

There is a hidden, yet important benefit of maintaining a "let go" list. If done right, it will speed up your decisions. This is because you will generally put things in the "let go" list because these items are in conflict with your value system. A well articulated "let go" list therefore helps you live your life based on your values. This automatically helps speed up your decisions.

SUGGESTIONS FOR YOUR "TO THINK" LIST

1. What are three things on your "To Think" list for your "to think" time this week?
2. Create your first "Let Go" list with at least five items.

_____

_____

_____

_____

_____

_____

_____

_____

_____

_____

ONE KEY TAKEAWAY
FROM THIS SECTION:

CHOOSE THE AREA OF IMPACT:	☐ PERSONAL ☐ PROFESSIONAL ☐ BUSINESS

THE TAKEAWAY:

Pause, Reflect and Record: Go to Appendix I (The Reader ROI Calculator) and fill in the details for this section.

CRAFT THE RIGHT AND RELEVANT STORIES

[6-MINUTE READ]

In a time of crisis, there will be an outpouring of stories. Some are fake, but most others carry the same information with varying levels of drama quotient.

If you are not guarded, these "dramatic" stories will have a profound negative effect on you. You have to protect yourself from being taken advantage of by that. However, on the other hand, you should not miss out on the opportunity to take advantage of the power of stories to help you gain and maintain attention from those you want to serve during the times of crisis.

All else being equal, the person who tells better stories will always win.

THE STORIES NEED TO BE M.O.V.I.N.G.

This is the time to collect stories right from your childhood days to until today where either you are the only person involved in the story, you were the lead, you were part of the team or you were behind-the-scenes helping others create the story.

For starters, put your stories in these categories:

1 **M**eaningful: Your work created more meaning in this world. For example, as part of your voluntary work, you organized a health camp to help people in 15 rural villages in a span of one month.

2. **O**ut-of-the-ordinary: You created magic – it could be an academic accomplishment that could be termed as jaw-dropping for those around you. Or, it could be some record-breaking sports achievement. Or, it could be something nobody with your background able to accomplish until you did it.

3.**V**alue-creating: This is plain and simple – you played a major role in one or more projects that created measurable value (usually financial in nature so that nobody has an objection)

4. **Insightful:** This is where you bring one or more "aha-moments" to the people around you. You may have created a framework or an approach that was fresh or you undertook a study that resulted in uncovering something of greater value.

5. **New:** This is all about innovation. It could be that you created or modified a process or a technique to get results faster or cheaper or both.

6. **Game-changing:** This category is for accomplishments that span far wider than the scope where you were operating. You were working in a startup, but what you were creating was changing the way an entire industry was operating.

The exercise above will help in many ways - most importantly in building your self-esteem. You need a healthy level of self-esteem and inner confidence to weather through a storm like the one we are witnessing now.

You might say I am just an employee in a large company, so I don't get to "play" like others. If so, here are some scenarios to think about:

- Do you have a story that will show some characteristics that people respect such as integrity, tenacity, and persistence?
- Do you have a story about how you saved a million dollars for your employer?
- Do you have a story about how you made a million dollars

for your employer?

- Do you have a story about how you unlocked a new market for your employer?
- Do you have a story about how you helped your employer get noticed by mainstream media?

Really, what about be the case or situation you are in, think about the following question:

WHAT IS THE STORY ABOUT YOU THAT IS WORTH GETTING PUBLISHED IN THE NEW YORK TIMES OR WASHINGTON POST?

If you have an answer to the last question, then you should have already been telling your story to the world.

If not, you should engage yourself in projects that will let you have such a story in the near future.

You need an "above-the-fold" story that showcases you at your best and shows how you can create opportunities for others.

Thank you for playing along with me by going down your memory lane. In all honesty, you don't need to be on the cover of the New York Times or Washington Post to survive and thrive in this environment. But, imagine the kind of personal growth you will experience when you embark on a journey that is supposed to get you there because you made a contribution that is so big they can't ignore you anymore.

RELEVANCE = RESULTS

Sometimes, it's that simple.

If there is no relevance, you can extend the logic above, there will be hardly any results.

Your stories definitely have to be relevant or else they only have entertainment value - nothing else.

Here is a simple technique to remember

1. **Notice first:** Observe others who are telling good stories. You learn from great teachers. Even if you don't want to pay someone to teach you to tell stories, you can watch TV, read books and blogs, and attend theater. You will notice that there are a lot of people out there who are great storytellers. You can be entertained or you can start noticing and learning from them.

2. **Practice next:** Watch the results of your own storytelling. It's all in the results. For example, if you tell a great product story that repeatedly makes sales, then you know that you are telling a good story. If you tell good stories, but they are not resulting in sales, well, you can blame the product or you can question your storytelling. You have to fix the problem one way or the other.

POSITION YOURSELF SO THAT THEY PUT YOU IN THE RIGHT BOX

People talk about ADD (Attention Deficit Disorder) as if it's a disease. I think in the new world, it is more a trait than a disorder. Nobody has time to listen to everything you have to say. They want to "box" you as soon as possible. They want to know where you fit in. Your elevator pitch will play an important role in determining what "box" they put you in.

"What box they put you in determines what opportunities they open up for you"

You might ask, why should we place so much importance on the box? The answer is simple. What box they place you in determines what opportunities they open up for you. If they think that you are a software developer, the opportunities they think up for you will be very different than those they think up if you are an entrepreneur.

Since the story you tell makes a huge difference, you have to place a huge importance on the art and craft of storytelling. In their classic book "Made to Stick", authors Chip and Dan Heath talk about ideas that stick, and one of the key components for making ideas stick is the stories behind them.

Here's what they say:

"We tell stories. Firefighters naturally swap stories after every fire, and by doing so they multiply their experience. After years of hearing stories, they have a richer, more complete mental catalogue of critical situations they might confront during a fire and the appropriate responses to those situations. Research shows that mentally rehearsing a situation helps us perform better when we encounter that situation in the physical environment. Similarly, hearing stories acts as a kind of mental flight simulator, preparing us to respond more quickly and effectively."

TO MOVE PEOPLE, START WHERE THEY ARE...

One of the greatest copywriters, Robert Collier said, "Enter the conversation that is going on in your prospect's head."

You have to first acknowledge what is going on in your prospect's head. It could be the uncertainty that they are experiencing, or it might be the overwhelm they are facing. Only when you acknowledge what they are going through, will they feel like you have understood them. Only when they feel understood will they lend their attention to understand what you are promising them through your stories.

So, in summary, here are the high-level steps to move people through storytelling:

Meet them where they are: Wherever your prospects are, you have to go there first. This is by acknowledging what they are seeing and feeling.

Make them discover their strengths: During times of crisis, people panic and they even forget about their core strengths.

Let them know that you understand their constraints: Know what their roadblocks are to get wherever they want to get to. This is a way to address their objections before they even bring this up

Provide proof that you are qualified to help them: Any kind of social proof that shows that you have been there and done that will help them become comfortable with you.

Present a story that is believable: Your story has to show them the path in clear terms – one where they take advantage of their strengths, has already factored in their constraints, and with your help, how they can see themselves going from where they are to where they want to go.

In a period of crisis like this, you move ahead if you know

995.

A WELL CRAFTED STORY HAS THE POWER to Convert a "WANT" INTO a "NEED" WITHIN A MATTER of SECONDS!

SOURCE: WWW.NAPKINSIGHTS.COM/NAPKIN/995/

how to make people move ahead. Some of the concepts you learned in this section will help you get started.

SUGGESTIONS FOR YOUR
"TO THINK" LIST

1. Put down your elevator pitch in terms of the person you want to serve, the problem you want to solve, and the promise you want to make, on a post-it note (Yes, a post-it note. After all, constraints spark creativity. Try it!)

_____

_____

_____

_____

_____

_____

_____

_____

_____

_____

_____

_____

_____

_____

_____

_____

_____

_____

_____

_____

ONE KEY TAKEAWAY
FROM THIS SECTION:

CHOOSE THE AREA OF IMPACT:

☐ PERSONAL
☐ PROFESSIONAL
☐ BUSINESS

THE TAKEAWAY:

Pause, Reflect and Record: Go to Appendix I (The Reader ROI Calculator) and fill in the details for this section.

GIVE AND GET THE RIGHT HELP THE RIGHT WAY

[7-MINUTE READ]

Giving and getting help is an art that is very important whatever be the times. However, during tough times, it becomes critical that you are very good at giving and getting help.

The order is important too. Notice, the title of this chapter is not "getting and giving help."

This is one of those areas where people don't pay much attention until someone like a mentor points it out to them.

Why?

Because, in general, when you don't get the results you were looking for, you tend to optimize the tactics that were employed rather than looking at the flaws in the fundamentals that are at the foundation. This is a blind spot to watch out for.

Let's get back to the core topic.

Giving and getting good help is also at the foundation of building meaningful long-term relationships. The right way to do both of the above should become your second nature.

If you try to give help in areas that are not your strengths, you and the person who is receiving the help will suffer.

Similarly, if you ask for help from someone in the area of their weakness, the help you might get is useless and you would have also wasted the person's time.

When I talk about this topic, most people raise their eyebrows. Some openly say, "I didn't know that there is an art and science to seek and give help. It seems like common sense to me."

What they are trying to say is, "I am complicating a very simple thing in life – giving and getting help."

I respectfully disagree.

This chapter will establish the relevant background for the topic and provide a few ideas on how to get better at this fundamental skill that each one of us should develop.

It is common knowledge that we all need help every now and then. However, most people try to solve their problems all alone. The concept of getting help for this group is generally called "Googling."

Let's cover the first aspect of **giving help.**

Someone calls you up for help and if you have the time available, you usually end up helping them. If you don't have the time available, you respectfully decline to help.

I just wish that life was this simple. This would be true only in a perfect imaginary world.

In the real world, well, it's a bit more complicated.

So, here is what (in some combination) may happen when you receive a request for help:

- You are already maxed out with your commitments so you don't have time.
- The request was made in an area where you don't have a lot of expertise or authority.
- You feel that the requester is unduly taking advantage of you.
- You feel that the requester is using you as a crutch.
- You are not confident that you can satisfy the requester with the way you fulfill the request.
- You think that fulfilling the request will be a thankless job.

Simply put, you may be the only person the requester has approached for help but you may have many such requests from many individuals. Do you now see the complexity of the problem?

There is no simple solution for this complex situation. Here are a few things to consider before you jump to provide that help:

Commit to diagnose first: If you are in a hurry, you may think that you can save time by just offering the help that has been requested. Most often, you will be wrong. Typically, the person requesting the help will have thought of a solution and is coming to you for help to put the solution in place. If the person's diagnosis of the underlying problem is not right, the solution won't be right and you helping them won't solve the underlying problem. So, if you are rushing, all you can promise is that you will think about all of your prior commitments at hand and see if you can fit in their request. In reality, you are buying time to diagnose the request and the problem so that you know it's worth your time.

Look at the forest: Every small commitment when looked at in isolation will seem easy to fulfill. It is the sum total of all the commitments that will cause you to slip. So take great care before you say "Yes" to those seemingly small commitments. It is better to say "No" than to sign up and fail to deliver.

Leverage your network: It may take you a few hours to fulfill a request but the same request may be fulfilled by someone in your network within minutes.

The million-dollar question is, "Do you know how to find that 'right' someone and is your relationship with them strong enough to request help?"

What compelling reasons can you provide someone in your network to set aside time to fulfill this request?

A powerful network used right can increase your capacity to offer help and In turn can make your network more powerful.

Teach people to get the most out of you: Your behavior always sends a message to other people. You are constantly teaching others how to treat you. You can also make a conscious effort to teach others how to get the most out of you by letting people know where your true strengths are.

You are, in effect, teaching them when to come to you for help. When you are operating in the areas of your strengths, fulfilling requests is relatively easy.

Teach them to fish: Even when you can solve the problem, it is best to spend some time to help the requester help themselves.

Remember the old saying, "Give a man a fish and you feed him for a day; teach him how to fish and you feed him for a lifetime."

Now, let me focus on getting help.

Life would be simple (and too easy, in my opinion) if we could get to the "right" people when we need help and, they immediately drop whatever they are doing and come to our rescue. Unfortunately, that can only happen in fairy tales or movies. It is far from reality.

So, what can we do to get the help when we need it the most?

No.
1046

TO BOOST LEVERAGE, DEVELOP the CAPACITY to RAPIDLY DEVELOP the CAPACITY of OTHERS to MAKE a DIFFERENCE !

SOURCE: WWW.NAPKINSIGHTS.COM/NAPKIN/1046/

Here is a simple approach to consider.

Contribute early and frequently: There is one rule that has always helped me. If you want to be successful, please help others become successful. Early in your careers (and always), your goal has to be to contribute and be an opportunity to other people. Do as many favors as possible as early as possible in your career.

Build your emotional bank account: Everyone knows about the power of reciprocation but rarely do people use it wisely. You give and you get. The order is important and the intention is important too.

You have to give first before you can get: You will "get" for sure but it may not be from the same person to whom you gave. You are building your emotional bank account by giving. You may be able to withdraw from this bank account at a later date. Obviously, you can only withdraw if there is sufficient balance in the account.

Extend your network far and wide: With the attitude and approach outlined in the first two items, it should not be hard for you to extend your network far and wide. However, building your network and long-term relationships do not happen by accident.

You need to put in a conscious effort. Think about the last conference or a networking event that you attended. How many cards did you collect? More importantly, of the cards that you collected, with how many have you followed up and established a relationship?

Your power is directly proportional to your network. It is also not how many people you know, but how you know these people. How much credibility have you built with them?

How is building a strong network relevant to getting help? The stronger your network, the easier it is to make a request for help.

Build your personal brand: In the previous section, we talked about the importance of "how" you know the people. Personal branding looks at a different metric. How many people know you?

Your personal brand, simply put, is your promise to the world and the marketplace.

Whether you want it or not, you have a personal brand. Whether it is powerful enough is something that you have to determine for yourself.

You can't build a powerful personal brand overnight but once you build it, you have shortcuts for many things in life. In this context, **more importantly, you will see that your requests will be treated as priority if you have a powerful personal brand.**

Craft your request for help: This, I think is the most important part of getting help. The quality and the speed with which you will receive help will depend on how you craft your request for help.

This is more of a strategy than a tactic. In fact, if you employ a tactical approach to this, your request will probably fail. **The basic premise on which your request has to be based is not on what you want to get done but on what the other person will get by fulfilling the request.**

So, think about this. Can you craft your request in such a way that the other person feels you are doing him a favor by asking him to fulfill this request?

If you can do that, you can be rest assured that you will get help whenever you want for the simple reason that you are focusing on the other person rather than yourself.

It's worth repeating that for what you want to get done, your goal is now to find out that person who will benefit the most by doing that work for you.

Is that easy?

No.

Can it be done?

You bet!

SUGGESTIONS FOR YOUR "TO THINK" LIST

1. What are your top three strengths?
2. Craft a request for help with someone in your network that will make them want to thank you for considering them for this.

_____

_____

_____

_____

_____

_____

_____

_____

_____

_____

_____

_____

_____

_____

ONE KEY TAKEAWAY
FROM THIS SECTION:

CHOOSE THE AREA OF IMPACT:	☐ PERSONAL ☐ PROFESSIONAL ☐ BUSINESS

THE TAKEAWAY:

Pause, Reflect and Record: Go to Appendix I (The Reader ROI Calculator) and fill in the details for this section.

INSTITUTE A "NO INSIGHT LEFT BEHIND" POLICY

[5-MINUTE READ]

Let me make a bold claim here. If you forget everything you have read or you will read in this book and focus on just understanding and practicing the "no insight left behind" policy, your growth is guaranteed irrespective of what the external circumstances are.

The reason there is an abundance of sensational news everywhere around you is because that's how the media thrives – create fear, uncertainty, and doubt to keep people on the edge and bring them back again and again.

Your attention is their asset and they will do whatever it takes to get it and keep it to serve their interests.

Even if you shy away from news, conversations with friends and family will keep initiating you into these topics. Only you can force an "early quit" on those conversations and bring them back to topics that matter most to you.

Where should we go instead of sensational news?

What is the alternative?

Go where there is curated information from people who have been there and done that – not people who think they are experts, but those that are actually real experts.

Now, here comes the important point. What do you do with the insights you are acquiring from the various sources?

This is where I say that you should institute a **"no insight left behind" policy.**

I will give you some background for the same.

A few days ago, one of my mentees posed a question. "What would be a strategy that will most likely help me gain an unfair advantage in the coming year?"

Rather than making up an answer right away, I chose to reflect on it a bit. I jotted down a few ideas, tested several of them with a few smart friends, and finally chose this one.

Yes, this is my final answer (as of now at least).

The strategy is to operate with a mindset to not leave any insight behind.

I have been operating with the above principle for ages, but someone had to ask a question to bring that to the surface.

INSIGHTS ARE PLENTY

Finding knowledge and insights is easy. You can find them via smart friends. You can find them at libraries. You can find them on the web. You can find them at conferences.

This can go on and on.

If collecting insights is your quest, you are in luck.

BUT, YOU RARELY GET
READY-MADE ANSWERS

However, internalizing those insights and applying them to a specific context is hard work. It requires serious effort.

In most cases, people encounter an insight and walk away from it. Or, they walk towards finding the next insight.

Sometimes the quest may simply be to look for ready-made answers that will tell you exactly what to do. You may be looking for the available options to deal with a particular situation and you probably want to know which is the best among available options.

The problem?

It rarely works that way.

There is magic in application. They say ideas are dime a dozen for a reason.

Insights are the same.

If you don't adapt and apply the insights in your context, they are reduced to some form of intellectual entertainment.

Mostly useless.

However, adapting and applying is magical because if you succeed, you can reap the rewards from the results and if you don't succeed, you learn and grow.

There is a limit.

Of course, you can't possibly try to take advantage of every insight you encounter.

Nobody can.

It's not even practical.

So, it seems like we have a dilemma. You want to operate with a mindset that you don't want to leave any insight behind. But it's practically impossible to make use of every insight you encounter.

Well, not really a dilemma if you come at it from a different vantage point.

THE GAME-CHANGING MOVE

If you expand the space of possibilities for a new insight to projects of people that matter the most to you, more magic happens.

Here is a simple process to consider:

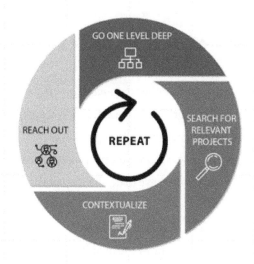

A. GO ONE LEVEL DEEP

Every time you encounter an insight, rather than rushing to the next one, stop and reflect on other uses for the insight.

To what other places can this insight bring a positive impact?

Just engaging in this part of the exercise alone will yield more benefits than simply consuming an insight.

B. SEARCH FOR RELEVANT PROJECTS

Now, search for relevant projects within the network of people that matter the most to you and who might benefit from this newly encountered insight. If you have a good handle on what projects your network is engaged in, this should be an easy thing to do.

C. CONTEXTUALIZE

This step is important. Rather than just throwing an insight to someone in your network, walk the extra mile. Contextualize the relevance of the new insight to their project(s).

If that insight was relevant to multiple projects for multiple people in your network, you have to do this step multiple times.

D. REACH OUT

Now, reach out to each one of the people in the above list to share the insight in the context of one or more of their projects. The medium (in-person, phone, email, etc.) is not as important as the completeness (insight + context) of sharing.

If you get this part right, the other person will feel they received a gift from you.

E. REPEAT

Depending on your time availability, you can repeat this for as many insights you encounter.

Here is an example:

The first time I read a paper on effectuation by Prof. Saras Saraswathy, I fell in love with it. While traditional thinking is all about assembling the right resources to reach your goal, effectual thinking is about finding the right goals to reach, with the already available resources. Good entrepreneurs need both kinds of thinking.

When I see that someone in my network will benefit from Prof. Saraswathy's work, all it requires is for me to send this PDF with a few lines to set the context.

It's that simple.

Over the last five years, I must have sent this out to a few hundred budding entrepreneurs.

Insights are the same, contexts are different.

Practicing the no insight left behind concept is also a gift you give yourself. You sharpen your thinking every time you apply an insight to make it work in multiple contexts.

SUGGESTIONS FOR YOUR
"TO THINK" LIST

1. Take a recent insight that you got from a book or a mentor. Run through the 5 steps (Go one level deep, search for relevant projects, contextualize, reach out, and repeat).

_____

_____

_____

_____

_____

_____

_____

_____

_____

_____

_____

_____

_____

_____

_____

_____

_____

_____

_____

ONE KEY TAKEAWAY
FROM THIS SECTION:

**CHOOSE THE
AREA OF IMPACT:**

☐ PERSONAL
☐ PROFESSIONAL
☐ BUSINESS

THE TAKEAWAY:

Pause, Reflect and Record: Go to Appendix I (The Reader ROI Calculator) and fill in the details for this section.

SELF-CARE IS NOT SELFISH, LACK OF IT IS BEING IRRESPONSIBLE

[2-MINUTE READ]

We talked about giving and getting help and the need to have a posture to serve. However, there is a limit. You cannot serve at the expense of neglecting self-care.

Why?

There are many reasons; here are a few:

#1. You are important. Without you, there is no vehicle to serve others.

#2. Your capacity to serve increases if you don't have to

worry about breaking down with your own problems.

#3. If you need a lot of help because you ignored taking care of yourself, you are adding the burden on your loved ones.

#4. You need to serve as an example of what to do and not as an example of what not to do.

Remember the classic airline announcement goes like this, "Wear your oxygen mask before you help another person with it." The same logic applies even outside the context of airline travel.

When times are tough, there is an increase in the number of requests for help. As we discussed earlier, each of the requests on its own will seem small, but the collective burden on you will be enormous if you don't have a method to handle all of these requests gracefully.

Lack of self-care is being irresponsible to yourself and your loved ones. If your speed of reinvention is lower than the speed of change at which the world is evolving, you will be at a competitive disadvantage sooner rather than later. And, as mentioned earlier, in case of a personal breakdown, you are robbing the already diminished capacity of your loved ones to care for you. When you look at it from this lens, lack of self-care seems to be the selfish act – not the other way around.

MANAGE YOUR EGO

934

WHEN the EGO occupies the "HOME" of the MIND, it LEAVES NO ROOM for SELF IMPROVEMENT!

(for the wrong reasons!)

SOURCE: WWW.NAPKINSIGHTS.COM/NAPKIN/934/

What has ego got to do with self-care?

A lot.

Your ego can come not only in the way of your own improvement, but also comes in the way of taking care of yourself. When the ego starts managing you, you will think that you are invincible and think that you can take your body for granted. Nothing would be far from the truth.

Check your ego before you wreck your health.

SUGGESTIONS FOR YOUR "TO THINK" LIST

1. How are you taking care of your "self" on a daily basis?
2. How are you holding yourself accountable for this practice?

_____

_____

_____

_____

_____

_____

_____

_____

_____

_____

_____

_____

_____

_____

_____

_____

_____

_____

_____

_____

_____

ONE KEY TAKEAWAY
FROM THIS SECTION:

**CHOOSE THE
AREA OF IMPACT:**

☐ PERSONAL
☐ PROFESSIONAL
☐ BUSINESS

THE TAKEAWAY:

Pause, Reflect and Record: Go to Appendix I (The Reader
ROI Calculator) and fill in the details for this section.

ESCAPE FROM THE PRISON CELL-HOPPING GAME

[3-MINUTE READ]

Think of an imaginary game called prison cell-hopping. The idea here is simple. You are in an imaginary prison cell. You don't like it, but after some time, you get used to it. Not that you are happy there, but you can tolerate the stay there.

Someone around you teaches a game called prison cell-hopping. It is a lame game, but they make it look like super fun. The rules are simple. You leave your prison cell and move into another prison cell temporarily. When it comes to inconvenience, this prison cell is no different from the previous prison cell, but there is a difference – this prison cell is different. But the "being different" difference won't cut it for too long.

So, what do you do?

You engage in one more edition of prison cell-hopping.

What happens there?

History repeats. You are happy at the beginning for a short while, get back to the default mode very soon, and then what do you do?

Yes, you got it. You engage in prison cell-hopping again.

Then, one day it dawns on you that prison cell-hopping is not taking you out of the prison, it is just taking you to another cell in the same prison.

Duh!

It's a wake up call.

I know you are glad that it's a fictional story.

Before you celebrate, just think again.

You may be one of those people who are engaged in prison cell-hopping, the only difference is that you are just playing this game within your head.

Let me explain.

Whenever you start worrying about the things that you have no control over, you are in a prison cell.

Whenever you are unhappy that someone else did not change, you are in a prison cell.

Whenever you are jealous that someone else got ahead, you are in a prison cell.

Whenever you wish to get ahead without getting your hands dirty, you are in a prison cell.

Whenever you crave for a prize without paying the price, you are in a prison cell.

When you claim credit for someone's work, you are in a prison cell.

When you don't show gratitude for the gifts of goodness, you are in a prison cell.

When you use fear as an excuse for inaction, you are in a prison cell.

When you deliver mediocre work with any excuse, you are in a prison cell.

When you let your ego stop you from learning, you are in a prison cell.

I can go on and on but you get the idea.

Observe the above and you will notice that none of the items have any upside, but all of them have a variety of downsides.

If you engage in the game of prison cell-hopping, you experience an internal change of environment, but it is a phantom relief because all you did is to go from one meaningless prison cell to another.

If you want to escape from this dangerous game, you need to raise your self-awareness and revisit your worldviews, biases, values, and beliefs. This can be triggered by something you read or by someone you trust when either of them shake you up to wake you from a self-induced intellectual coma.

The key is to notice the clues that will be in plenty. A clue typically manifests itself in the form of capacity depletion to delay in getting things done. It may manifest itself in the form of a goal post shifting further away from you. It might also appear in the form of frustration because you are putting in the effort, but results seem to be meaningless.

Being mature means having the ability to notice and acknowledge the clues objectively and not dismiss them because you are clouded by your emotions.

You will pay a big price if you continue to play the prison cell-hopping game. During a crisis, you will pay even more because you need all of your capacity to deal with the crisis; there is no time or capacity to waste. It is urgent for you to escape from playing the prison cell-hopping game.

SUGGESTIONS FOR YOUR "TO THINK" LIST

1. What does the prison cell-hopping game mean to you?
2. How will you ensure that you don't engage in playing a prison cell-hopping game in the future?

_____

_____

_____

_____

_____

_____

_____

_____

_____

_____

_____

_____

_____

_____

_____

_____

_____

_____

_____

_____

ONE KEY TAKEAWAY
FROM THIS SECTION:

**CHOOSE THE
AREA OF IMPACT:**

☐ PERSONAL
☐ PROFESSIONAL
☐ BUSINESS

THE TAKEAWAY:

Pause, Reflect and Record: Go to Appendix I (The Reader ROI Calculator) and fill in the details for this section.

PART 3

REBOUND STARTER KIT

It is tempting to now look for a recipe – a step by step approach to guarantee success. First, there would be none and second, even expecting one is an indication that we have not yet understood the gravity of the situation. So, here it is: We are now witnessing the societal operating system upgrade to fit the new reality. Programming on the new operating system has to wait until the upgrade is complete.

So, what could you do?

You pursue your mastery in adaptive thinking and agile execution. This is the need of the hour. In this section, you will find a few approaches and frameworks to consider as you get ready to take on the challenges ahead.

LEARN TO INFLUENCE IN THE WORLD OF MVT

[5-MINUTE READ]

MVT, as I explained before, is **M**inimum **V**iable **T**ouch. This may be the world we will live in for some time to come.

There are a class of people who are called digital nomads. They do most of their work online and travel from one place to another every few months or every few years. Obviously, they don't meet their clients in-person, but wherever they are located, they do meet with their fellow digital nomads. This way, they strengthen their bonds with the global, loosely coupled tribe they belong to.

In the MVT world, there may be a situation where we will have to mimic certain parts of the digital nomad life. We might have to learn how they engage with people on various projects.

It will be hard to imagine how we can learn, live, love, work, and leave a legacy in the MVT world, but a few years from now, we all will have changed and embraced what will be the new normal.

At the foundation of surviving and thriving in the MVT world is your ability to influence one or more people at a time to get their buy-in for making progress with what matters most to you. If you are a veteran internet marketer who has been doing this for decades, this new world of MVT is not a problem for you. If not, there is no time to waste; get cracking on adjusting to the MVT world.

THE SEROTONIN FIX

A warm hug or a handshake releases the chemical serotonin within you and the person you just met. Serotonin acts as a mood enhancer and helps with giving the meeting get a head start on a graceful note.

In the MVT world, there is no handshake or a hug.

So, right there, you are at a disadvantage when you shift everything online.

But, if you are willing to invest in yourself, you can get that serotonin fix through an alternative means, through your eyes and your words.

If you choose to replace an in-person meeting with a video call, you still can express your warmth through your eyes. If you master the language and narrative, you can increase the odds of providing that serotonin fix.

The serotonin fix is one example of a subtle change that you need to pay attention to.

I don't know your background or your ambition, but you know all about you. So, think about your own situation, on how you used to connect with people the very first time. And then, how you were building on those relationships.

With MVT in place, what exactly do you have to change so that this connection and subsequent relationship building activities have no speed breakers in sight?

If there is one other element that you must focus on, it is your zero-eth impression.

THE ZERO-ETH IMPRESSION

There is a saying that you don't get a second chance to make a first impression. There is no question about the importance of the first impression, but there is one more aspect that probably takes an even more important role – that is the zero-eth impression.

Zero-eth impression is nothing but what the other person thinks of you based on all the information they have collected about you from the internet and social media. This information may be what you have shared, for example on your blog, on

YouTube, on social media channels, or the information could have been sourced from people that are mutual connections.

The zero-eth impression silently colors the first impression. How?

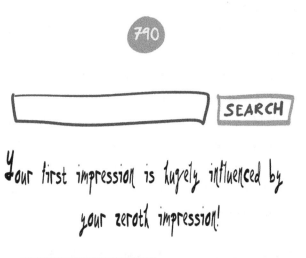

Your first impression is hugely influenced by your zeroth impression!

SOURCE: WWW.NAPKINSIGHTS.COM/NAPKIN/790

The zero-eth impression creates an image of your personality even before they meet you for the first time. For the first few minutes of your first meeting, they are busy calibrating you against the image they have of you from the zero-eth impression.

So, what's the problem?

Again, this is very subtle. If they get the feeling that you are not very confident, they will pick up every small thing that strengthens their original conclusion (however faulty it is) and ignore the evidence that will prove otherwise.

Unless you are totally authentic (your first impression matches the zero-eth impression), it will be a hard time to get through to the other person.

If this was the pre-MVT world, imagine how much more care you need to put in the world where MVT is the new normal.

Pay extra attention to craft your zero-eth impression because it's a necessity, not a luxury in the world of MVT.

LET YOUR HEARTS HUG EACH OTHER

In the days of social isolation, how do you get the human contact that all of us dearly need? How do you touch without touching?

You may not be comfortable with a hug or close contact at this time, but that should not prevent you from letting your hearts hug each other!

One of my super-smart and progressive teachers, Maria Kellis (mariakellis.com) taught me the concept of "heart-bridging". In short, it is a technique she developed and enhanced, that helps you connect deeply with any other person (however far they are) by creating an imaginary bridge from your heart into their heart. Maria describes heart bridging as follows:

Heart bridging is a deep heart connection that brings a new level of connection and awareness. It allows you to feel and merge together in love, as love, through love. You can simply think of it as a new level of "touching". We are used to thinking of touching as a physical connection, yet we can be close to each other and feel that connection without actually touching physically. This is the easiest way to build this bridge. There is a reason that we congregate together in places or sit next to each other. We intuitively feel the presence of the other person even when we are not touching them. We know that the other person is there. We feel them, with our hearts. This tool of heart bridging allows you to extend this awareness.

So how can you build a "heart bridge"? Let's start with the few simple steps that Maria teaches. Find a person close to you that you can practice building a bridge with. You can practice that with a family member or a member of your household to start with. Use all your senses to perceive more than just the physical body or shape of the person you want to "touch" and feel that connection deepening. Imagine that you have a bridge that you are building. Imagine the bridge. What does it look like? Do you hear any sounds or do you smell any smells? What does that bridge look like? As you are imagining the bridge the bridge appears because energy goes where attention goes. Even if you think that nothing has happened you should be able to feel the difference. It feels like a deeper, truer, committed connection. Often when people connect with Maria teaching this bridge for the first time they start crying and they always ask why that is? It is because there is so much love there when we can feel that deep level of connection then we are in fact connected, truly. What you achieve with this bridge is not only to feel the other person's heart, you are also going to feel your own heart more deeply.

The next step is to build bridges over longer distances. Imagine that you could "bend" time and space in your mind. You don't actually have to do anything, except to use your imagination. Imagine that you can in fact bring the person that you are thinking of closer to you, and imagine that everything is merged and concentrated into this one moment in time. Everything is happening Here and Now. Use your imagination to "see" the person you want to build a bridge to right in front of you and imagine that you are connecting a bridge from their heart to your heart, the same way you would have done with the person in the room before. If you can feel that connection in your heart, congratulations. You have successfully built a heart bridge. If you cannot feel it yet, then you can see a video of Maria demonstrating this simple technique on our website and giving you tips (link). Maria has been practicing and teaching this technique for decades so it might just be easier to build a bridge with her techniques as she describes them in the video.

Try this and you will immediately find a deeper connection.

DON'T SQUANDER THE COGNITIVE SURPLUS

Here is the biggest upside that you might overlook – the cognitive surplus that is handed out to everyone.

Think about it – less commute, more time at home, eating healthy – all lead to more time for yourself to think, plan, and execute.

But, here is the problem. If you are not thoughtful, you will totally squander it. You will regret it later, but by that time, it's too late to do anything about it.

In the busy life you lead, it is rare to get an opportunity to encounter cognitive surplus of this magnitude ever again.

Open up your idea notebook or those bucket list projects that you wanted to pursue and fill your calendar with them before you get inundated with mindless news and other sensational stuff.

A tip if you want to take it. Start any project during this period with at least one more partner-in-crime even if the other person is not required and you can take this project to completion all on your own. The partner-in-crime will automatically act as an accountability partner and will stop you from sliding away from the project. It's like an insurance policy against project defaults.

ONE KEY TAKEAWAY
FROM THIS SECTION:

**CHOOSE THE
AREA OF IMPACT:**

☐ PERSONAL
☐ PROFESSIONAL
☐ BUSINESS

THE TAKEAWAY:

Pause, Reflect and Record: Go to Appendix I (The Reader ROI Calculator) and fill in the details for this section.

OBSERVE THE CHANGING CONCERNS AND BREAKDOWNS

[4-MINUTE READ]

My philosophy teacher, Toby Hecht first shared the concept of concerns and breakdowns and since that day, my worldview about people shifted in an irreversible fashion.

People always act to take care of their concerns or fix the breakdowns that happen while taking care of their concerns.

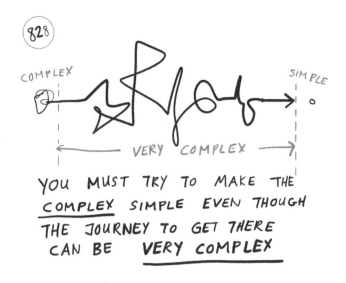

YOU MUST TRY TO MAKE THE COMPLEX SIMPLE EVEN THOUGH THE JOURNEY TO GET THERE CAN BE **VERY COMPLEX**

SOURCE: WWW.NAPKINSIGHTS.COM/NAPKIN/828

Understanding this will make comprehending really complex human behaviour reasonably simple.

Concerns can be put into two broad buckets: personal and professional. They may come in various forms or flavors, but the approach is always going to be the same:

1. Act to take care of a concern
2. Encounter one or more breakdowns along the way
3. Act to handle these breakdowns on their own or with the help of someone (sometimes for free and sometimes for a fee)

4.   Repeat

When any major change happens (for example, a game-changing innovation), there is a change of concerns and breakdowns – sometimes in a small way and sometimes in a big way depending on the quantum of change at play.

For example, before the printing press was invented, one of the concerns was preserving and distributing knowledge. When the printing press was invented, that concern was addressed.

But, not for long. The new concern was ease of access to that knowledge. Then came the internet, where all this knowledge was stored. This concern too was thus addressed.

But, not for long. The new concern was speed of access to that knowledge. Then came the search engines and portals, addressing that concern.

The next major concern was the need for ubiquitous access. People wanted knowledge at the push of a button wherever they were and whenever they wanted. Then came smartphones and apps. Ubiquitous access was thus sorted out.

I can go on and on about this, or we can pick another topic and you can watch the migration of concerns and breakdowns.

If you observe, the phenomenon goes both ways on the convenience scale. There is always a migration of concerns; breakdowns occur when something becomes more convenient or when something becomes more inconvenient.

An innovation moves the world towards more convenience.

A crisis moves the world towards more inconvenience.

But, the result at a human level is the same – change of concerns and breakdowns.

If you want to spot possibilities, you have to become a keen observer of the change of concerns and breakdowns. This helps you start at the fundamentals and you won't be chasing someone else with some solution, but you'll be chasing them down to improve their lives.

Without a deep understanding of concerns and breakdowns, you wouldn't know what people care about. If you don't know what people care about, you can't come up with an offer that is meaningful and relevant to them. If you can't come up with a meaningful and relevant offer, nobody will pay you anything because a money transaction happens as part of a value exchange.

The same logic of concerns and breakdowns applies to businesses as well.

Still want proof?

Look inside of yourself.

Replay the story so far of your own life. See how there was an ongoing migration of concerns and breakdowns throughout your life journey. In fact, every time there was an inflection point, the concerns and breakdowns changed instantly.

Keeping this in mind, you can either do this exercise yourself or with the help of a mentor for a segment of people or for a vertical, a particular geography, a particular demographic or a combination of the above. You can also add your own criteria.

The goal here is to find the market segment that you are

passionate to serve with their need for the newly migrated concerns and breakdowns.

THE NUANCE THAT MATTERS

There is a subtle nuance that you need to pay attention to. Sometimes, the core concern might remain the same, but what changed is how people want to take care of that concern and how urgently they want to take care of it. As you dig deeper, take a few more minutes to ask the "how" and the "how urgent" questions. It will help in crafting your offer to the marketplace.

This approach is foolproof, be it in the post-COVID world or beyond.

Always remember that genuine curiosity may get you a prize, but lack of it in areas that matter most to you will make you pay a price.

SUGGESTIONS FOR YOUR "TO THINK" LIST

1. What important problem do you solve for your clients?
2. What all has changed in relation to the above in the new environment?

_____

_____

_____

_____

_____

_____

_____

_____

_____

_____

_____

_____

_____

_____

_____

_____

_____

_____

_____

ONE KEY TAKEAWAY
FROM THIS SECTION:

**CHOOSE THE
AREA OF IMPACT:**

☐ PERSONAL
☐ PROFESSIONAL
☐ BUSINESS

THE TAKEAWAY:

Pause, Reflect and Record: Go to Appendix I (The Reader
ROI Calculator) and fill in the details for this section.

BECOME A MERCHANT OF POSSIBILITIES TO CREATE VALUE

[12-MINUTE READ]

"Chaos gives birth to dancing stars."

- FRIEDRICH NIETZSCHE

The bad news first. If you look for problems, you will find them.

The good news next. If you look for possibilities, you will find them too.

The choice is yours.

Note: Looking for problems does not necessarily constitute negative thinking. It is actually positive thinking when you are looking for problems with the noble intention of solving them.

First of all, rarely will someone hand you a "golden" possibility. If that was the case for everyone, it wouldn't be called a "golden" possibility anymore. If you ever get the feeling of being entitled to an opportunity, you can eliminate that thought to avoid future frustration and misery.

In that sense, the title of this article is misleading a bit because you typically don't spot a possibility. You create one. OK, technicalities and semantics aside, how do you spot or create possibilities?

Here are some ideas to consider:

1. LOOK FOR GAPS

Let's take the context of an organization for the sake of this discussion.

The organization structure where you work is typically a set of neatly arranged boxes. Every box represents a department focusing on a particular set of activities within the organization. The boxes are connected so that the work flows between these different departments. Between these boxes are the "golden" gaps. In other words, between the departmental work lies some more work that's important but nobody currently owns that work. This is your chance to take ownership of that work and fill the gap or seize the possibility.

You can extend the approach even outside the organizational context.

2. LOOK FOR MORE RESPONSIBILITY

More responsibility will generally involve more work but it's more about being accountable for bigger results. Just like the rich people get richer, the people who produce bigger results are given more opportunities to produce even bigger results. This means you are automatically put in a vantage point to spot new possibilities.

3. LOOK FOR BIGGER PROBLEMS

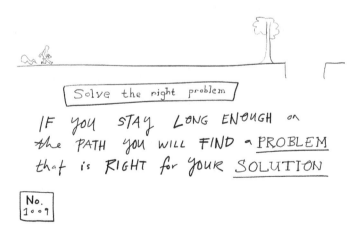

Solve the right problem

IF YOU STAY LONG ENOUGH on the PATH YOU WILL FIND a PROBLEM that is RIGHT for YOUR SOLUTION

No. 1009

SOURCE: WWW.NAPKINSIGHTS.COM/NAPKIN/1009/

Our general tendency is to stay away from problems and stay farther away from bigger problems. However, if you are not solving a big enough problem, chances are that you may not be doing anything important. If you are not doing anything important, then chances are that you may not find any opportunities. When many people stay away from a big problem, you need to buck the trend and go after it.

Look around and see what is the big problem around you. Try to find a way to get engaged, to lead, or be in the team to solve this problem. Solving a bigger problem typically would mean seizing a bigger opportunity.

4. LOOK FOR KNOWLEDGE ARBITRAGE

Knowledge arbitrage is a term coined by Gary Hamel. In simple terms, it is a process of applying knowledge from one field to another field. Remember Netflix for renting movies and the same way remember NetJets for renting corporate jets. How about Avelle for renting luxury handbags? Do you see the power of knowledge arbitrage?

Go beyond your company, industry and/or trade. Look elsewhere in an unrelated field and see what's working. See if you can apply that in your company, industry and/or trade.

5. LOOK FOR RELATIONSHIP NETWORK ARBITRAGE

Relationship network arbitrage is very similar to knowledge arbitrage but happens across multiple personal or professional networks you belong to. Most smart people who are connectors have these three things in common - (a) they belong to multiple personal and professional networks and (b) they are genuinely curious and (c) they care as if it's their own problem.

If you are one of those people, you will notice that you will be sort of "relevant resource" rich in terms of knowledge, connections or both. When someone is facing a challenge or pursuing an opportunity, you can immediately do a mental scan across all your networks and see if there was some knowledge or some connections or both and you will start looking at making those connections usually expanding the possibilities for all involved.

6. LOOK TO LISTEN

Yes, it seems simple but most people don't listen. Barry Grieder from Landmark Forum says it nicely, "We don't listen. Either we are talking or we are waiting to talk again." When you actively listen with an open mind, you will start spotting possibilities sooner rather than later.

Frameworks for Structured Possibility Engineering

Now more than ever, we need to get back to the first principles. This is where tried and tested frameworks come in handy.

My friend DP "Sri" Sridhar runs an Innovation Consulting company called TruNorth (www.trunorth.ai) through which he routinely engineers new possibilities for his clients globally. I had a long conversation with Sri on the current situation and the path forward to create new possibilities. Sri picked a couple of frameworks from his framework arsenal that could help you streamline the uncovering of new possibilities.

Here they are:

1.   Past-Present-Future Framework (PPF)
2.   The Landscape Framework

THE PAST-PRESENT-FUTURE FRAMEWORK

This framework helps one to look at a challenge in its present form, reflect on the past to see if a similar challenge existed and if yes, how it was resolved and to extrapolate how a similar challenge might manifest in the future.

Considering the COVID-19 situation, we could apply this framework to ask a few questions.

What have we learned from past events, be it the Spanish Flu or the Plague?

What is stopping Artificial Intelligence from predicting the occurrence of such an event?

What would it take for the medical fraternity to be on top of such events?

THE LANDSCAPE FRAMEWORK

This framework will help you look at the ecosystem play. Let us understand this with an example.

If Zoom/Webex is the system, all that has gone into building this product – the software, the algorithms, the hardware – are all subsystems. The internet, the browser, audience are all part of the supersystem.

So, when we combine the PPF Framework with the Landscape Framework, we get something like this:

	Present
Supersystem	Users, Internet, Browser
System	Zoom Video Conference
Subsystem	Software, Algorithms, Hardware

So, what was there in the past?

In 1968, video conferencing was first introduced and packaged as a commercial solution at the World's Fair in New York. The technology introduced was called the Picturephone from AT&T. It was the first video telephone device designed for the mass where they could communicate 'via video' for 10 minutes at a time. This was a clunky start and a very expensive solution. It did not get a very favorable response until the introduction of systems from Compression Labs. These systems began to sell for $250,000 and the video conferencing system from PictureTel took a big price drop to $80,000 in the late 1980s, still making both seem much more attainable only to larger corporations.

In the 90's major advancements in IP technology, the internet and video compression enabled more possibilities for video collaboration via desktops. IBM took notice and dropped the price of their systems to $20,000 systems, while the introduction of CU-SeeMe (no audio) from Macintosh made video collaboration a bit more of a reality for consumers and businesses alike.

The late 1990s to the early 2000's, Polycom played a large role in the evolution of video conferencing with systems such as the ViewStation® in '98 that put Polycom at 1 billion in sales for the year and their desktop solution, Via Video which debuted in 2000.

Source: https://www.vyopta.com/blog/video-conferencing/brief-history-video-conferencing/

	Past
Supersystem	Dedicated Window, Desktop
System	Picturephone, CU-SeeMe, Polycom's ViewStation
Subsystem	Compression Labs, IP Tech

WHAT COULD BE THE FUTURE?

With the 6 foot world and the lockdown, IT companies now see a new ray of hope. TCS, with an employee count of 500,000, making it one of the biggest employers, aims to have only a 25% workforce in office by 2025, the rest are to work from home. Indian IT companies, which are the preferred outsourcing partners for Fortune 1000 companies, are evaluating whether their employees must return to the campus or continue to work from home.

What is the possibility here?

What kind of systems should we develop for a large workforce to stay connected and collaborate more effectively? How do we churn out new innovations that will work in remote settings? What should happen in the subsystem and how should a supersystem function for this to happen?

	Past	Present	Future
Supersystem	Dedicated Window, Desktop,	Users, Internet, Browser	Augmented Reality-enabled Devices
System	Picturephone, CU-SeeMe, Polycom's ViewStation	Zoom Video Conference	AR/VR-based Products
Subsystem	Compression Labs, IP Tech	Software, Algorithms, Hardware	AI/Deep Learning Algorithms

The dictionary defines a 'merchant' as one who sells.

In our current situation, will the COVID-19 phenomenon be the merchant? Will it sell us new ideas while we close our doors to old friends and neighbors? Will this merchant open windows to new possibilities?

It remains to be seen. Most results of this particular merchant's business will be seen in the near future rather than in the present.

THREE PIVOTS, MANY MORE TO COME

Right out of the gate, I saw two successful pivots and I am sure there are many more to come.

PIVOT #1: GENIUS NETWORK GOES VIRTUAL

Joe Polish is the founder of Genius Network. It's not a mastermind, but a connection network. In Joe's own words, "Any problem in the world can be solved by the right genius network." I am a fan of Joe and have been part of the Genius Network for a while.

Pre-COVID, the standard way was for a subset of members to meet 2 or 3 times a year at Joe's office at Phoenix for two days to network, learn and grow.

The routine for these two days was extremely well-organized and usually members go back with several $100K+ ideas to implement in their own businesses. In between these meetings, members could connect with each other and of course they always have access to a Genius Network portal with a treasure trove of information and insights.

With COVID-19 in full-swing, there was a clear disruption to the Genius Network business model. I have known Joe for more than a decade and if there is one person who is committing to providing a lot of value to anyone they come into contact with, it will be Joe topping the charts.

Joe and his team got to work almost immediately and turned the entire 2-day experience to go fully virtual.

I had the opportunity to witness the magic in action. We all logged into a Zoom session, listened to the organized talks, participated in Q&A while contributing and consuming wisdom continuously in the group chat. The "break out" rooms feature was fully utilized by bringing small groups of members to have a conversation about what was covered in the previous session.

Joe's team silently worked in the background to curate all the information (it was a LOT) that was shared on the chat and updated the member portal and where applicable also updated public portal as a way of caring for the public at large.

For Genius Network, when their traditional business model was threatened, the only way ahead was to use what's available (virtual solutions) to bring the same value as before.

And if you ask me about the ROI, I will say that it was even higher than before as there was ZERO incremental cost to participate in the experience.

PIVOT #2: GRATITUDE DINNERS GO VIRTUAL.

I met Chris Schempra recently through our mutual friend Mike Roderick. Chris is the founder of a company called 747Club. Chris and his girlfriend, Molly love cooking. So for years, they have organized what are called Gratitude Dinners, where they bring a curated group of people for dinner and conversations almost everyday. Chris has sparked over 400,000 relationships so far.

Chris has a really interesting ice-breaker technique. (You can adopt this, but please give Chris due credit for his brilliance.) Here it is:

In general, "Tell us about yourself" is rarely a good ice-breaker. Because some people will be too detailed and some will be too brief.

Chris starts all the Gratitude Dinners with a question (I am paraphrasing here) like below:

If you could give credit or thanks to one person in your life that you don't give enough credit or thanks to, who would that be?

A slight variation that my friend Arun Nithyanandam suggested is as follows:

Who is the one person who has made such a big impact on your life that even if you thanked him or her everyday for the rest of your life, it won't be enough?

Whichever version you choose, I am sure you will notice the

power of the question. It will immediately bring out a story of gratitude for the person who was responsible for probably the biggest transformation in their life. In parallel, they will share their own story of transformation.

When I shared this with my son Sumukh, he said that the answer to the question also brings out how the narrator has been helped before and in turn provides clues as to how else others can help him or her.

One question leads to many wonders.

The problem here was the same. COVID-19 immediately put a stop to their core offering, Gratitude Dinners.

What did Chris and Molly do? They went virtual.

How in the world can a dinner go virtual, you might ask.

Participants bring their own dinner and join a virtual meeting. I was one of the 26 participants attending the dinner through Zoom - the other participants were mostly strangers. By the time the meeting ended, many of the participants had become acquaintances and many more had become friends. That was the power of the Gratitude Dinner even when it was virtual.

PIVOT #3 FROM HIGH-TOUCH TO A REMOTE VIA MINDSET SHIFT

When my friend Jade Connelly Duggan shared the story of how Kate, an acupuncture practitioner pivoted her business,

I was intrigued because, well, acupuncture is a high-touch business and it's not easy to pivot.

Here is Kate's pivot story.

Kate Quinn Stewart runs Nurturing Spirit Acupuncture, a one-woman operation in Washington, DC. She had been practicing acupuncture for the last 15 years. For the five years before that, she was a massage therapist. In short, Kate had spent her entire career in high-touch professions, working one-on-one with her clients and patients to support them in healing from a wide range of physical, mental, and emotional issues.

Suddenly, with the arrival of the novel coronavirus and the announcement of local stay-at-home orders, protecting the health of her patients and her community meant closing her office doors to in-person visits.

Kate had reached, supposedly, an **inflection point** - something radical had to happen.

Determined to find a way to continue putting her skills to use for the benefit of her patients, Kate scrambled to gather the resources needed to start offering telemedicine. She knew that her patients approached her because they wanted to feel better. Maybe they had pain, or they couldn't sleep, or felt frustrated and unmotivated – they just wanted someone to listen and to help them feel better in a safe and natural way.

Something Kate had learned years ago from her teachers came to the rescue.

Kate had always known that the medicine lived within each of her patients. She was just a catalyst to reawaken that medicine, to reconnect her patients with their own innate healing potential. She had learned that everyone's body wants to be well and is powerful enough to regulate and repair itself, given the right conditions.

So with both nervousness and a sense of excitement and possibility, Kate started using every other tool she had collected over her years of study in the realms of massage, reflexology, Chinese medicine theory, nutrition, qi gong, breathwork, meditation, aromatherapy, psychology, and neuroscience. Her last day in the office was March 12, 2020 and within four days, Kate was leading her first virtual wellness sessions, guiding each of her patients through a custom-tailored experience to help them shift into whatever new feeling state they were seeking.

Where before Kate had sometimes leaned on her needles to do most of the work, keeping her intention for the treatment to herself and just letting her patients lie down quietly and "have the experience," now she engaged her patients much more fully in the treatment process. Chinese medicine theory is filled with metaphor and poetry, explaining the inner workings of the human body in terms of the elements, seasons, and transformations that we witness in the natural world. As her patients described their struggles, Kate would use this intuitive, metaphorical language to explain to them what was happening inside, which gave them a new sense of perspective on their own experience.

She began to guide her patients through self-acupressure treatments, explaining the particular nature of each point and how it could serve as a portal to some virtue, strength, or self-healing capacity that lay within them. She encouraged them to really tune into themselves, attending to the sensation at a particular point, noticing their own responses to different practices. She led them through explorations and reflections on their inner landscapes, reminding them of their innate power, beauty, and strength. "That point belongs to you now. That practice is yours to call on whenever you need it. That sense of peace and comfort is something your mind and body are capable of producing. You can always come back to that state," she would say.

With one patient who was experiencing dizziness accompanied by a sense of confusion and overwhelm, Kate instructed her to massage a point near the ankle that empowers clear vision and perspective. Together, they envisioned hiking through the woods to an expansive overlook where they could get a panoramic view of the surrounding territory. They both felt transported, and the patient's dizziness faded, replaced by a sense of clarity and calm.

With another patient experiencing intense anxiety, Kate guided her to massage a point that is known for calming fears, explaining that this point represented the "inner sandbags" she needed to keep the river of her fear from flooding its banks. Her anxiety soon disappeared and there was only a sense of calm.

With both Kate and her patient co-creating a vision for how each part of the treatment served to support that patient's desired outcomes, the virtual sessions came alive in a powerful way. Her patients were surprised at how effective the work was, even without the needles, and they began to feel more empowered to create their own shifts toward health. When they knew they couldn't just wait around for their next needle treatment to lie down and get up feeling better, they began to implement what they learned in their virtual sessions. Reliably, they would report back that when symptoms arose, they knew what to do and were able to shift how they were feeling. And that shift was really what they were coming to acupuncture for all along.

Inspired by this success, Kate is now working to develop online courses so that she can bring the techniques she has been using in her virtual wellness sessions to a wider audience

The above three pivots happened right in front of my eyes within the first few weeks of the COVID-19 outbreak. There are many more to come for sure.

ONE KEY TAKEAWAY
FROM THIS SECTION:

CHOOSE THE AREA OF IMPACT:	☐ PERSONAL ☐ PROFESSIONAL ☐ BUSINESS

THE TAKEAWAY:

Pause, Reflect and Record: Go to Appendix I (The Reader ROI Calculator) and fill in the details for this section.

THINK HUNGER ALIGNMENT, FRICTIONLESS ALCHEMY AND LONG-VIEW CHOREOGRAPHY

[5-MINUTE READ]

If you want to pursue something big, you have to show up with your heart and soul.

80 %. of life may be showing up.
But, don't forget the other 20% of
taking action to contribute where you
showed up.

SOURCE: WWW.NAPKINSIGHTS.COM/NAPKIN/444

But, that's not enough. It is almost impossible to do it all by yourself. The opposite is also true. If you complete your dream project all by yourself, then that dream may not be something big after all.

Note that you don't have to go for something big from scratch. You can combine or blend together different pieces in a fashion where there is a mutual win for everyone involved.

Next, you have to find people who are competent and more importantly hungry to grow and by being a member of your dream project, they should see their individual growth speed up.

Once the project begins, you need to be able to organize work in such a way that all members are playing the roles in which they have maximum opportunity to use their "super powers".

If you got so far, you already know the concepts of hunger alignment, frictionless alchemy and long-view choreography.

Let us look at each of the terms in more detail.

HUNGER ALIGNMENT

When there is a deep hunger for what a particular outcome will provide, the person does not need a pep talk to walk the extra mile. He or she will gladly do it, not just because it's the right thing for the project at hand, but because it's the right thing for them.

If you are trustworthy and close to someone, the person might reveal what they are hungry for and "why they are doing what they are doing".

But, there are only a finite number of people who can be super close to you.

So, how do you find out what someone is hungry for when all you have had are a few meetings with them?

Answer: You need to piece that together in combination of the three things below:

- By listening deeply to what is said and what is not being said
- By watching their actions as they go about with their pursuits
- By looking at how they got to where they are today

So, what can you do when you find out someone's hunger to be something or to get somewhere?

Well, now you have to see whether you can carve out a role in your project for them with a powerful narrative that will make them conclude that it is in their best interest to participate in it as it is aligned with their hunger.

It is important to not directly state the connection but keep the narrative in such a way that they conclude that it's best for them. They are way more committed if the decision to participate originates from them.

The concept of hunger alignment is also important when you are connecting two people. If you are thoughtful in the connection, you can ensure that in the narrative to each one of them, you will bring about how connecting to the other person is good for them. Again, you have to let them conclude about hunger alignment for themselves and not hear that from you.

FRICTIONLESS ALCHEMY

The original definition of alchemy is here:

"The medieval forerunner of chemistry, based on the supposed transformation of matter. It was concerned particularly with attempts to convert base metals into gold or to find a universal elixir."

In this context, alchemy means you are bringing together various resources to harvest the "gold" from the combination.

Frictionless alchemy is an arrangement where you ensure

that individual components (typically people) that are part of the alchemy do not create friction that will derail or delay the outcome that you are looking for.

To increase the odds of frictionless alchemy, you have to focus on the selection before the project initiation rather than an intervention post the start of the project.

If you think it's no big deal, you may be brushing away the real problem at hand.

Your selection at any point in time is only limited to the best among available options for you to select from.

Think about it again.

Do you see it?

THIS is the real problem.

Your available options.

Yes, the available options form the superset of what you can select. That is limited by both your capacity to afford and the obligations you have created with a set of people through generosity and caring for them when they needed that the most.

The power of reciprocation makes people walk the extra mile as if it's a walk in the park. If you have not made that investment in them way before you need them, then the relationship is reduced to maths.

When it comes to relationships, it's chemistry that wins over maths any time.

So, the golden rule is to contribute at every available opportunity, but consume only when convenient to them.

LONG-VIEW CHOREOGRAPHY

Now coming to the execution. I borrowed the word choreography from the world of arts. Imagine watching a well-executed dance ensemble. It's like magic.

A well-executed project looks precisely like that.

What has the term long-view got to do with choreography?

It's about relationships and how you view them.

In my view, there are only three kinds of relationships:

1. Long-term

2. Very long-term

3. Lifetime

When everyone who is involved knows that you view the relationship either as a very long-term or a lifetime level, the engagement in the current project will be at a level beyond the ordinary.

Choreography comes into play when you empower the various participants and put them into roles where everyone gets to play to their strengths (most of the time).

Remember that there will be problems and challenges along the way, like any other project. But, when people are clear that the span of your relationship with them is above and beyond this particular project, they try to set their ego aside and fix problems. Because that's how people act if they are committed to a very long-term or lifetime relationship. If this was pure transactional arrangement, typically people have little or no wiggle room on their stand.

So, here is how they all come together - when you think about it, you can't afford to master these skills to thrive in the post-COVID world:

Hunger alignment will ensure that every participant in the project is involved because participating in this project has an added benefit directly providing value to the pursuit of their dreams or indirectly helping them increase their capacity to pursue their dreams.

Frictionless alchemy will ensure that team members are chosen to ensure that everybody respects each other for the value they bring to the project and collectively there is a focus to make the project a masterpiece rather than locally winning for their individual glory.

Longview choreography ensures that while the focus is to make this project a masterpiece, your relationship with the individuals participating in the project extends beyond this project. This in turn makes everyone yearning to win this project even more. Done right, you will also help more people take on a longer view of the relationships that are building amongst the participants in the project helping them to each win big later in their lives.

Now, your situation may be that you are not in a leadership position so should you bother about hunger alignment, frictionless alchemy and long view choreography.

The answer is Yes, you cannot ignore this. Here are a few reasons:

- You may not have the title of a leader or a manager. That

should not stop you from leading or more initiatives within your company. That's how you build yourself up to become a leader

- You may not be leading a project at work, but you are surely managing your own personal projects. You can put to use the ideas

- If you are working on a non-profit project, you can still use these concepts to make a bigger impact

- Every project you work on using these concepts has multiple benefits - you will strengthen your execution muscles and you will increase the depth of your relationships - it's the best of both worlds.

SUGGESTIONS FOR YOUR "TO THINK" LIST

1. List three people who you can help get to where they want to go.
2. How can you partner with them or get paid to give that help?

_____

_____

_____

_____

_____

_____

_____

_____

_____

_____

_____

_____

_____

_____

_____

_____

_____

_____

_____

_____

ONE KEY TAKEAWAY
FROM THIS SECTION:

CHOOSE THE AREA OF IMPACT:	☐ PERSONAL ☐ PROFESSIONAL ☐ BUSINESS

THE TAKEAWAY:

Pause, Reflect and Record: Go to Appendix I (The Reader ROI Calculator) and fill in the details for this section.

EXTEND THE VALUE CHAIN RATHER THAN STARTING FROM SCRATCH

[4-MINUTE READ]

Let me take a business example to make a point

When a crisis like COVID-19 hits, it is common for most businesses to go into self-preservation mode. This means they won't start anything new. So, if you sense that's what is happening, you need to stop trying to make them embrace anything new. It probably won't work.

However, they may be open and actually looking forward to making something existing better and more efficient. This is where you can use "extending the value chain" as a wedge to get inside.

This is where the concept of "extending the value chain" can help you.

I first read about value chain extensions from Adrian Slywotzky, the author of "The Art of Profitability" and many other books.

Years later, I still remember the specific case study about extending the value chain. The case in point was a company called Cardinal Health. One of the offerings from Cardinal Health was the sale of surgical equipment to hospitals. Everything was going well until Chinese manufacturers entered the market and started selling similar equipment for a fraction of the cost. At those price points, it was impossible for Cardinal Health to compete.

They had to do something.

The solution was value chain extension.

I won't go into all the details, but here is the final solution. You will see the power of value chain extension immediately.

With the newly designed solution, hospitals had to maintain zero inventory of surgical equipment. On the day of a surgery, less than thirty minutes before the operation, a package would arrive at the operating room with a tray full of surgical equipment exactly the way the surgeon wanted it to be placed, including the choice of the brand that he/she preferred. It was completely personalized, just-in-time service offered at a premium by Cardinal Health.

There was no chance for the Chinese manufacturers to compete with a newly designed offer; it was like comparing apples to oranges.

Cardinal Health won.

In reality, the concept of value chain extension won big.

The kind of disruption that will be at play will require you to take a hard look at the value chains that you are engaged in.

Look at what exactly happens before, during and after the current mode of value delivery at this time.

What could you expand in the scope of what you do either before or after your current scope of engagement?

How could you reimagine what you do so that who you serve gets 5x or 10x the value they are getting now?

THE SPEEDBREAKER (THAT IS NOT)

YOU CAN WORK AS HARD AS YOU WANT, BUT THE MARKETPLACE WILL ONLY REWARD YOU FOR THE VALUE YOU HAVE CREATED !

When I share this idea with my students (these are usually first-time entrepreneurs), the general push back is that they don't want to lose their focus. They also feel that they may just not be experts in every aspect of the value chain. In other words, they have a brilliant excuse for why this may not work.

In reality, this is an example of another blindspot.

In order to extend the value chain, you alone don't have to be the expert in all aspects of the solution. You can bring smart partnerships and stitch together something awesome that will make their customer's day.

This is a double-win because the end customer gets the benefit of a fully integrated solution and the smart partners you bring into the deal will thank you for expanding their footprint.

EXPANDED LISTENING HAS TO BE AT THE FOUNDATION

When you serve your customer, you will probably focus your conversations within the scope of what you are serving them. That boundary is at best imaginary as there is nothing stopping you from expanding the conversations on either sides of the value delivery.

Questions like, "What else has to happen within your organization for us to succeed with this project?" and/or "What other related projects are you excited about?" will elicit a response that will provide clues for value chain extension.

Granted, not everything you hear from the customer will

lead to a value chain extension opportunity, but if you shy away from collecting inputs on related areas, then there is no chance of spotting one or more possibilities.

When you expand your scope of listening to topics beyond your current focus, ensure that you are not distracted so much that you lose focus on fulfilling the promise you made to them. Value chain extension has to be additive, not a substitution.

Now, let us think how you can apply this in your professional or personal life.

If you are working in a company, your employer is a business too. Your employer will think like any other business - act very conservatively and drop all the new projects. Don't think only external vendors will get affected. Every employee's value and contribution in the past will be assessed. Plus, based on their future direction of the company, every employee's potential contribution for the future of the company will also be assessed. With this in the back of your mind, think about the "extending the value chain" model for projects within your own company. You will not only start growing, but also stand out easily.

SUGGESTIONS FOR YOUR
"TO THINK" LIST

1. What happens before and after my services at our clients?
2. How can I collaborate with others to integrate their offerings to provide a more comprehensive solution to our clients?

_____

_____

_____

_____

_____

_____

_____

_____

_____

_____

_____

_____

_____

_____

_____

_____

_____

_____

_____

ONE KEY TAKEAWAY
FROM THIS SECTION:

CHOOSE THE AREA OF IMPACT:	☐ PERSONAL ☐ PROFESSIONAL ☐ BUSINESS

THE TAKEAWAY:

Pause, Reflect and Record: Go to Appendix I (The Reader ROI Calculator) and fill in the details for this section.

PRACTICE DELIVERING RESULTS IN ADVANCE

[3-MINUTE READ]

When we start working in a world where the bias has moved from "trust first, suspect later" to "suspect first, trust later", you have to consider changing how you make the first move towards engaging in a professional relationship.

Dean Jackson and Joe Polish talk about a method called Results in Advance where you produce outcomes that are of value to someone with whom you want to engage, before reaching out to them with a potential business arrangement.

This will also create a much better zero-eth impression (what comes way before the first impression) and sets the bias to engage than to find a reason to not engage.

Think about it.

Here is one approach:

When you want to engage with someone, you typically go to them with a promise that you will either deliver or help them get an outcome that they are in pursuit of. They have to agree to compensate you based on that promise. In many cases, if the outcome is not completely clear and air tight, you are asking for compensation based on the promise and your best efforts to get that outcome.

Those whom you engage with might be thinking what the odds of you helping with that outcome are and whether they can get a good ROI at the level of compensation you are asking for.

You point to historical accomplishments and ask them to draw parallels to build confidence on your capability.

Sometimes it works, but most of the time it won't because it's usually an apples to oranges comparison. Both parties know that past performance is not an indicator of future success. Times have changed too.

You need a better proxy to make it easy.

That's why the Results in Advance is sort of a fool-proof alternative.

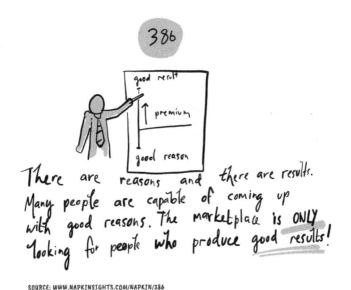

SOURCE: WWW.NAPKININSIGHTS.COM/NAPKIN/386

When you produce results in advance, the velocity of dealmaking shoots through the roof. The traditional doubts about whether you can make it happen will go away. The focus completely shifts on the quantum of compensation that is on the proposal. If that is reasonable and affordable, then what remains is signing on the dotted line.

THE ADD-ON ADVANTAGE

There is an add-on advantage that is subtle, but important. When you go with a Results in Advance approach, you immediately create two things:

a)   A pattern interrupt and

b)   Shift in the criteria of comparison

Pattern Interrupt: This approach interrupts the pattern they are seeing with all others who come with a promise and a story about why they will succeed in delivering on that promise. This is where you create an advantage by going to them with some proof that will give them way more confidence on what's to come.

Shift in the criteria of comparison: The criteria of comparing your offer with that of others at hand becomes both interesting and a bit confusing in a good way. You come with some proof and others come with a compelling promise. The two sides are not equal however, and you slice and dice it. This agan tilts the balance in your favor.

However you see it, there is only upside with the Results in Advance approach. There is more work involved compared to just going with a compelling promise. But, the extra effort is worth it as it immediately translates into an increase in the velocity of deal-making.

THE STRATEGY THAT RARELY FAILS

If there is one strategy that rarely fails, it will be to "care deep and serve right" especially when they most need you.

Here is a real-life story that makes this point and more.

Dino Watt and team serve a niche - they help orthodontists across the United states to build their businesses. When COVID-19 hit the world with a vengeance, Dino and team made a radical decision - they went to all their clients and said that they will continue to serve them as before (and maybe with even more intensity) with only one catch - they would do it for free. Dino's point was that his clients needed to take care of their employees first before they paid their advisors. Dino also knew that his clients needed him most during this period where confusion and chaos was the order of the day.

If Dino continued to charge them as earlier, most of them would have no choice but to cut that off to save their employees. When that happens they would lose access to some wise advice exactly during the time when they could not afford to miss that kind of advice to navigate stormy waters.

So, the bold decision was to let go of tens of thousands of dollars in revenue per month to **care deep and serve his clients right** when they needed him most.

In other words, what Dino and team set out to do was to produce results in advance for their clients when the world changed (see Dino's write up on "The World stopped for you" in the next section)

The reactions to Dino's offer was all over the place, but if there was one word that could sum that up - it was gratitude. Every one of the clients appreciated Dino's offer. Dino and team probably put in way more hours than when they were getting paid for their services.

There is another thing that Dino did. He went to fifteen other consultants (some of them could be considered competitors) in the same industry and convinced them to give their best stuff for free by participating in free Facebook Live events with him.

Dino also conducted a straight 8 hour online event mainly educating participants from across the industry (whether they were Dino's clients or not) with the only goal of serving anyone and everyone.

One of the prospects reached out to Dino said, "Dino, I had never heard of you before, but now I am following everything you do"

Only time will tell what is the return on Dino's generosity, but I have a feeling that it would be pretty awesome.

ONE KEY TAKEAWAY
FROM THIS SECTION:

CHOOSE THE AREA OF IMPACT:	☐ PERSONAL ☐ PROFESSIONAL ☐ BUSINESS

THE TAKEAWAY:

Pause, Reflect and Record: Go to Appendix I (The Reader ROI Calculator) and fill in the details for this section.

PART 4

REFRAME AND CHARGE AHEAD

REMEMBER THE FUNDAMENTAL REFRAME

[5-MINUTE READ]

There is no reason to panic or get frustrated with all the coming changes because nobody wins an argument with reality.

THE TIME YOU WASTED **WISHING** YOUR PAST WAS DIFFERENT, IS THE TIME YOU LOST FOR PLANNING A WINNING FUTURE!

SOURCE: WWW.NAPKINSIGHTS.COM/NAPKIN/810

Remember that you get tired when you argue with reality, but if you accept and take advantage of reality, you get rich – not only in terms of money but in all aspects such as fulfillment in life and a sense of meaning.

Also, you already know this - there is no absolute reality. But, there is your version of reality, your truth or your perception. This is neither good nor bad on it's own, but you should never forget that because it is "your" reality, you CAN probably do something about it.

For starters you can transform your reality via what is called a reframe – conveniently turning it into what may be a disadvantage into an advantage for you.

While someone sees a problem and gets worried, an entrepreneur might look at it and see a possibility for him. The entrepreneur just reframed that problem into a possibility.

Dino Watt is a fellow member of the Genius Network community. He is an author and a relationship expert who helps people be more proactive, productive and profitable in all areas of their life. What he wrote below is a brilliant example of a reframe at multiple levels:

THE WORLD STOPPED FOR YOU.

The world stopped for you to **focus** on what is important.

The world stopped for you to **embrace** not being in control.

The world stopped for you **rethink** the way you do business.

The world stopped for you to **dedicate** more time with those you love.

The world stopped for you to **connect** with what you really want in life.

The world stopped for you to **remember** how good it feels to be creative.

The world stopped for you to **desire** more connection with your neighbors.

The world stopped for you to **notice** the things that have become mundane.

The world stopped for you to **learn** the power of prayer and spiritual connection.

The world stopped for you to **create** memories in your

home, instead of on a trip.

The world stopped for you to **renew** your commitment to what you said you wanted.

The world stopped for you to **have more** gratitude for the things you took for granted.

The world stopped for you to **show** the world who you are, not just who you say you are.

The world stopped for you to **move** forward even if you don't have all the pieces figured out.

The world stopped for you to **hear** the beautiful sounds that have become white noise.

The world stopped for you to **let go** of the beliefs and habits that are not serving you.

The world stopped for you to **decide** to no longer wait until it's the "right time".

The world stopped for you to **build** friendships no matter the physical distance.

The world stopped for you to **recognize** how expensive overthinking can be.

The world stopped for you to **see** the beauty in your spouse's imperfections.

The world stopped for you to **take courage** in making that next bold move.

The world stopped for you to **strengthen** your relationship with yourself.

The world stopped for you to **pay attention** to that small voice inside.

The world stopped for you to **realize** that 'done' is better than perfect.

The world stopped for you to **commit** to being more intentional.

The world stopped for you to **organize** your spiritual house.

The world stopped for you to **step-up** and serve others.

The world stopped for you to **level up** your skill set.

The world stopped for you to **love** what is.

The world stopped for you...

If the above list makes you re-look at even one or two items from what Dino covered, you will already see a positive change.

Let's take the general scenario and split people into two categories: (a) people who need help and (b) people who can give help. For the sake of simplicity, let's keep the ratio as 50:50.

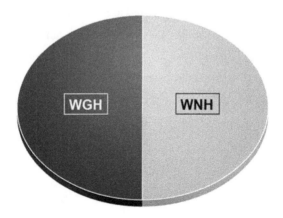

Now, during times of crisis like COVID-19, the ratio changes drastically, let's say to 10:90 – 10% of the people in the "who can give help" category and 90% of the people in the "who need help" category.

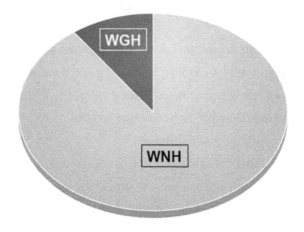

If you are in the segment of people "who need help", suddenly your world of possibilities shrinks as everyone around you struggles to make it work and are seeking for help which is rare to find, as the population of those who can give help has shrunk dramatically.

But, if you put yourself in the "who can give help" segment, your possibilities expand like never before.

That's an example of a reframe to see problems as possibilities

ONE KEY TAKEAWAY
FROM THIS SECTION:

**CHOOSE THE
AREA OF IMPACT:**

☐ PERSONAL
☐ PROFESSIONAL
☐ BUSINESS

THE TAKEAWAY:

Pause, Reflect and Record: Go to Appendix I (The Reader
ROI Calculator) and fill in the details for this section.

REFINE THE NARRATIVE FOR MORE POWER

[5-MINUTE READ]

The outlook you have about life, the story you tell yourself, the quality of questions you ask all will help in your journey to reinvention. Let us look at some of those in this section.

HAPPY MORNING!

When I got to learn about Mahatria and his work, one of the first things I noticed was how he and the people around him greeted each other.

Instead of "good morning", he would say "happy morning." It seems like a subtle change, but it's a powerful reframe to put back happiness in the stressed-out lives of people around us.

Try this as a start by changing your greetings to:

Happy morning or

Happy afternoon or

Happy evening

You might see some people raise their eyebrows the first time, but soon they will be "happy" to hear this.

THE DEFINING MOMENT IN THE MAKING

Every successful person has one or more stories about their defining moments that set them on a new trajectory towards reaching the heights of success.

I have had over a hundred conversations about defining moments of people who have accomplished amazing things. More than 80% of them had something in common. They all went through some obstacle that seemed insurmountable when they faced it. The obstacle did not disappear on its own. They grew their capacity so much that the obstacle no longer seemed insurmountable.

Interestingly, almost none of them felt that they were witnessing a defining moment when they encountered it. It was always a recollection from the past.

It does not have to be only this way. We can change the

defining moment from happening by default to created by design.

What if you look at the COVID phenomenon as the "defining moment in the making"?

Try it. You will instantly change the way you look at the world around you.

THE QUESTION THAT MADE THE DIFFERENCE

I heard this story long ago from Osho. As you will see soon, it is the power of reframing questions to get what you want.

This is a Sufi story.

There were two disciples learning from the same master. They were also close friends. Everyday they would meditate for hours inside the sanctum after which they would go to the garden for their walking meditation.

Both of them being smokers, they hatched a plan to ask the master for permission to smoke when they were in the garden. They thought it wouldn't be polite to smoke inside the house but it wouldn't be disrespectful if they smoked in the garden. They decided to seek the master's permission the next day.

The next day, they approached the master separately.

In the evening, when they started their walking meditation, one of the disciples took out his cigarette and started smoking. The other one was shocked and told the smoker that it's not wise to go against the master's orders.

The smoker was surprised and said that when he checked with the master, the master had given him permission to smoke.

Now, it was the first person's turn to not only be surprised but also be upset that the master had said "No" to him and had said "Yes" to his friend.

The smoker asked, "So what did you ask the master?"

The non-smoker said, "I asked whether I can smoke during walking meditation."

The smoker smiled and said, "Well, that explains it. I asked whether I can do my walking meditation while smoking?"

The way the non-smoker put the question made it look like there was a lack of dedication.

The way the smoker put the question made it look like he was walking the extra mile.

FOCUS ON THE SILVER LINING

There is a saying that every cloud has a silver lining. You probably know this, but because of all the noise around you, your focus is still on the dark cloud.

The COVID scenario might have changed a few things for you and the viable alternative may be sub-optimal compared to your earlier experiences. You are feeling bad about that and in that process, you might forget to look at what the positives are in the alternative method offered.

Here is a quick framework to look at:

What was the experience before?

What has changed?

What got missed because of the change?

What is the new alternative?

How can you reduce the impact of the change?

What new possibilities arise because of the change compared to earlier experiences?

How can you change the story to accentuate the positives?

Let us assume that you are a dance instructor and you teach dance in a couple of studios. Let us answer the above questions in this context.

WHAT WAS THE EXPERIENCE BEFORE?

Every week you teach about ten classes in three different studios. Your students love the ambience, the setting, the music system, and the camaraderie among fellow students. The pay is good and you enjoy the work because you love the craft.

WHAT HAS CHANGED?

COVID-19 happened. The studios are closed and there is no way to get 50+ students in one place. Naturally, all the classes are canceled. Your work is in jeopardy.

WHAT IS THE NEW ALTERNATIVE?

You design a program to teach dance online. Your students can join right from their homes. If anyone wishes to broadcast their videos, everyone gets the feeling that they are part of a community.

You make some adjustments to your garage and convert it into a temporary dance studio.

WHAT GOT MISSED BECAUSE OF THE CHANGE?

The studio setting, the congregation of students, the new friendships, the high-fives, hugs, and handshakes.

HOW CAN YOU REDUCE THE IMPACT OF THE CHANGE?

You create an online community to bring the connection aspect in some way.

WHAT NEW POSSIBILITIES ARISE BECAUSE OF THE CHANGE COMPARED TO YOUR EARLIER EXPERIENCE?

There are several:

- **CONVENIENCE:** Your students can participate right from their homes
- **SCALABILITY:** The total number of students per class is not limited by the studio size anymore
- **COST:** It costs you less in all respects, managing students to conducting classes
- **ENGAGEMENT:** At a studio setting, there was no need for an online community. Here, it's a must and you can engage with students at a whole new level

And more.

HOW CAN YOU CHANGE THE STORY TO ACCENTUATE THE POSITIVES?

Dance lessons right at your home everyday of the week.

Attend one class per week or all five of them – for a low price.

This is a very important distinction to bring forth – telling people that now they are getting a lot more value for their money compared to before.

ONE KEY TAKEAWAY
FROM THIS SECTION:

**CHOOSE THE
AREA OF IMPACT:**

☐ PERSONAL
☐ PROFESSIONAL
☐ BUSINESS

THE TAKEAWAY:

Pause, Reflect and Record: Go to Appendix I (The Reader ROI Calculator) and fill in the details for this section.

LEVERAGE THE VIRTUOUS CYCLE TO CHARGE AHEAD

[3-MINUTE READ]

Let us look at the core elements that come into play to make sense of this fast-changing world and to charge ahead. As you can see below, these elements may be categorized under skill set or mindset.

ANTICIPATION

Those who can read the world will have an edge over everyone else. If you can anticipate what's coming down the line, you can be more prepared and you will avoid rude awakenings. You can't build the anticipation muscle by being trapped in drama. You have to take the time to rise above the noise and watch what's happening around you with an objective eye. In addition, if you follow people who think deeply and provide unbiased analysis, you would have found a shortcut.

AWARENESS

This is the awareness to know and acknowledge what is happening around you. If you are busy running around like a headless chicken, life is a blur and there is no scope for taking notice of anything. Hence there will be a lack of awareness. Only when you slow down to stop, reflect and think, can you notice and be aware.

ATTITUDE

Attitude in short is your outlook and posture towards life. If you have a positive attitude, you will look for possibilities and if you have a negative attitude, you will look for problems. In either case, you will succeed in finding whatever you are looking for. The thing to be careful about is that your attitude is silent, invisible and internal; only you know what your attitude is and hence only you can take responsibility to cultivate the right attitude.

ACCEPTANCE

If you anticipate, be aware and have the right attitude, you will encounter reality in full force. At that time, there is one and only one thing to do. Accept it without blaming anyone and anything. We are here and by blaming anyone or anything, we cannot change the fact that we are here. Fighting against reality is futile. My friend and partner, Mike Martin says, "We can't fix what happened yesterday, but we are here and we can do something about tomorrow."

ARCHITECT

Alan Key said it brilliantly, "The best way to predict your future is to invent it."

The magic is to architect possibilities within the constraints of the current scenario.

You might find yourself crippled or helpless due to all the sensation and drama around you. But, you do have help.

Whether you know it or not, you have assets and you can leverage them. Here are a few assets to kickstart your thinking:

Your history: Everyone has a unique history, and nobody can repeat that one thing. You now have to see how you can leverage that history to make that asset relevant to the marketplace.

Your personal brand: Right now, you have a personal brand. It is your promise to the marketplace and the world.

Your relationships: Your connections, past and present (dating back to your college days or before) serve as assets. You need a strategy to leverage these relationships.

Your footprints: If you have traveled the world physically or through cyberspace, you have left your footprints. You can leverage these footprints and see where there is relevance.

Your story: Everyone has a story. I have one, and you have one too. How can you make your story interesting and relevant to the marketplace? That's the question you must address.

Your hunger and passion: Both hunger and passion are super important, but not visible.

ACTIVATION

Once you architect your plan (it could be a simple offer or a world dominating product), you have to get started. No meaningful outcome has come about with a brilliant plan that stays just on paper. An imperfect action trumps a perfect plan with no action.

AGILITY

The time is not right for making five year plans. This is the time to do a minimum viable plan and get going.

ADJUSTMENT

No plans, strategies and tactics can be set in stone. As you get feedback from the marketplace, you need to be open to revisit everything in light of the changed conditions and re-adjust everything on the table.

AUGMENTATION

This is about smart partnering. There is only so much you can do when you start from scratch. Together, everybody wins big.

AMPLIFICATION

When you know that you got something working right, you have to double-down on that and amplify to the maximum to make the most out of it.

ACCELERATION

If amplification is about reach, then acceleration is about velocity. Both these levers need to be cranked up to take advantage of what's working.

ACCOMPANY

This is the time to also shift your focus to those that are in need and lend them a helping hand. Not everyone's situation is good and by accompanying them to lift them, you will make your own journey more meaningful and fulfilling.

Then the cycle repeats. You go back to anticipation and re-work the steps.

ONE KEY TAKEAWAY
FROM THIS SECTION:

**CHOOSE THE
AREA OF IMPACT:**

☐ PERSONAL
☐ PROFESSIONAL
☐ BUSINESS

THE TAKEAWAY:

Pause, Reflect and Record: Go to Appendix I (The Reader ROI Calculator) and fill in the details for this section.

APPENDIX I:
THE READER ROI CALCULATOR

Remember, we learned that we should practice "no insight left behind" policy. Here is your opportunity to put what you learned to use and while you do that, calculate the ROI from the book + your effort to take meaningful action.

YOUR INVESTMENT:

(a)   Price you paid for the book: $_____

(b)   Time you took to read the book: _____ Hours

(c)   Your hourly rate: $_____

(d)   Cost for reading the book (b x c) = $_____

(e)   Opportunity cost (same as d) = $_____

(f)   Total cost (a + d + e) = $_____

YOUR RETURN:

INTRODUCTION: THIS TIME IT IS VERY DIFFERENT

You learned about the need for labeling anything right, because you start making assessments and taking actions based on the label. The first step is to see where else are you mis-labeling (people, opportunities etc.) at work and in your life.

TABLE 1:

	Amount in $
Value when applied to your life	
Value when applied to people in your network	
Total value (A)	

PART 2:
RENDEZVOUS WITH THE MANDATORY RESET

CHAPTER 1:
IT'S NOT THE RULES, IT'S THE GAME

You learned that the game has changed so mastering the previous game has no meaning or relevance. You also learned that playing the long game is a must.

TABLE 2:

	Amount in $
Value when applied to your life	
Value when applied to people in your network	
Total value (B)	

CHAPTER 2:
TO TOUCH OR NOT TO TOUCH –
LITERALLY AND FIGURATIVELY

You learned the second order and third order derivative problems and impact from practicing social distancing. What other areas in your life can you see the second and third derivative problems, opportunities and impact?

TABLE 2:

	Amount in $
Value when applied to your life	
Value when applied to people in your network	
Total value (C)	

CHAPTER 3:
RADICAL REINVENTION IS NOT A
LUXURY, BUT A NECESSITY

You learned about the need to reinvent yourself and your business. You also learned a key blindspot that might prevent you from reinventing, how to identify and fix it.

TABLE 3:

	Amount in $
Value when applied to your life	
Value when applied to people in your network	
Total value (D)	

CHAPTER 4:
NOT HIGHER INTENSITY, BUT
GREATER REIMAGINATION

You learned that the immediate temptation in a time of crisis is to increase the intensity of whatever you are doing even though you might know that this may not work, but you don't know any other way to respond. You learned that what you urgently need is reimagination. And you saw several examples of reimagination to provide you inspiration.

TABLE 4:

	Amount in $
Value when applied to your life	
Value when applied to people in your network	
Total value (E)	

CHAPTER 5:
9 UNCOMMON REASONS FOR THE RISE OF STRESS

You learned about 9 uncommon reasons for the rise of stress. It would be good to reflect on what might be the real reasons that you may be experiencing stress and what you could do to address them with what you already have.

TABLE5:

	Amount in $
Value when applied to your life	
Value when applied to people in your network	
Total value (F)	

PART 2 - RE-AMPLIFY THE FUNDAMENTALS

CHAPTER 6:
THE FUNDAMENTAL QUESTION

You learned about the difference between the postures for the question, "How can I find the next opportunity?" as compared to "How can I be an opportunity for someone else?"

TABLE 6:

	Amount in $
Value when applied to your life	
Value when applied to people in your network	
Total value (G)	

CHAPTER 7:
TO-THINK LISTS

You learned about the power of to-think lists. As a bonus, you also learned about the power of let-go lists.

TABLE 7:

	Amount in $
Value when applied to your life	
Value when applied to people in your network	
Total value (H)	

CHAPTER 8:
CRAFT THE RIGHT AND RELEVANT STORIES

You learned about the power of storytelling both for your personal use and for your business.

TABLE 8:

	Amount in $
Value when applied to your life	
Value when applied to people in your network	
Total value (I)	

CHAPTER 9:
GIVING AND GETTING HELP

You learned about the right way to give and get help. You also learned why this is the foundation for building long-term relationships.

TABLE 9:

	Amount in $
Value when applied to your life	
Value when applied to people in your network	
Total value (J)	

CHAPTER 10:
INSTITUTE A "NO INSIGHT LEFT BEHIND" POLICY

You learned about the framework to go from an insight to implementation, not once but multiple times to build your "value creation" muscle.

TABLE 10:

	Amount in $
Value when applied to your life	
Value when applied to people in your network	
Total value (K)	

CHAPTER 11:
SELF-CARE IS NOT SELFISH, LACK OF IT IS BEING IRRESPONSIBLE

You learned about the importance of self-care especially in times of crisis.

TABLE 11:

	Amount in $
Value when applied to your life	
Value when applied to people in your network	
Total value (L)	

CHAPTER 12:
THE URGENT NEED TO ESCAPE FROM PLAYING THE PRISON CELL-HOPPING GAME

You learned about the need to notice and acknowledge the dangers of playing the prison cell-hopping game and the urgent need to escape from it.

TABLE 12:

	Amount in $
Value when applied to your life	
Value when applied to people in your network	
Total value (M)	

PART 3:
REBOUND STARTER KIT

CHAPTER 13:
INFLUENCE IN THE WORLD
OF MVT

When the world moves towards Minimum Viable Touch (MVT), you need to unlearn the old ways of influence and start learning the new game of influence. You also learned about serotonin-fix, the importance of zero-eth impression, and heart-bridging. Lastly, you learned to recognize cognitive surplus and why you should not squander it.

TABLE 13:

	Amount in $
Value when applied to your life	
Value when applied to people in your network	
Total value (N)	

CHAPTER 14:
OBSERVE THE CHANGE OF
CONCERNS AND BREAKDOWNS

You learned why you need to be a keen observer of the change in people's concerns and the breakdowns associated with taking care of those concerns.

TABLE 14:

	Amount in $
Value when applied to your life	
Value when applied to people in your network	
Total value (O)	

CHAPTER 15:
BECOME A MERCHANT OF POSSIBILITIES

You learned five ideas to spot possibilities and two powerful frameworks to help with Structured Possibility Engineering.

TABLE 15:

	Amount in $
Value when applied to your life	
Value when applied to people in your network	
Total value (P)	

CHAPTER 16:
THINK HUNGER ALIGNMENT, FRICTIONLESS ALCHEMY AND LONG-VIEW CHOREOGRAPHY

You learned how to capitalize on hunger alignment, frictionless alchemy, and long-view choreography.

TABLE 16:

	Amount in $
Value when applied to your life	
Value when applied to people in your network	
Total value (Q)	

CHAPTER 17:
EXTEND THE VALUE CHAIN

You learned (with an example) about the power and possibility of value chain extension.

TABLE 17:

	Amount in $
Value when applied to your life	
Value when applied to people in your network	
Total value (R)	

CHAPTER 18:
PRACTICE DELIVERING RESULTS IN ADVANCE

You learned how you can stand out by simply choosing to deliver results in advance. You also learned two additional advantages of a) pattern interrupt and b) shift in criteria of comparison that comes with delivering results in advance.

TABLE 18:

	Amount in $
Value when applied to your life	
Value when applied to people in your network	
Total value (R)	

PART 4:
REFRAME AND CHARGE AHEAD

You learned the power of reframing starting with the fundamental reframe of going from WNH to WGH, the power of questions to reframe, happy morning, the making of the defining moment, and finally the virtuous cycle.

CHAPTER 19:
THE FUNDAMENTAL REFRAME

Here you learned about the fundamental reframe to see the people in the world as WNH and WGH and how you will see possibilities explode when you see yourself as belonging to WGH

TABLE 19:

	Amount in $
Value when applied to your life	
Value when applied to people in your network	
Total value (S)	

CHAPTER 20:
REFINE THE NARRATIVE FOR POWER

Here you learned how to refine the narrative for power - the language you use, the quality of questions and the outlook about life all will help you reinvent yourself to win in the new world.

TABLE:20

	Amount in $
Value when applied to your life	
Value when applied to people in your network	
Total value (T)	

CHAPTER 21:
THE VIRTUOUS CYCLE

Here you go through the virtuous cycle to recharge and move ahead.

TABLE:21

	Amount in $
Value when applied to your life	
Value when applied to people in your network	
Total value (U)	

Return Total Value = A+B+C+D+E+F+G+H+I+J+K+L+M+N+O+P+Q+R+S+T+U

Reader ROI = **(Return/Investment)*100**

ACKNOWLEDGEMENTS

The book is coming out at a crazy time. It was conceived, written, packaged, and published during the COVID-19 induced lockdown.

So many of my friends stepped in to help and it's hard to list them all out, but here are a few that walked the extra mile so they deserve a special mention:

- **Arun Nithyanandam**: for the overall flow and the name of the book
- **Ravi Char**: helping with naming the phenomenon as black bevy
- **Abhijeet Khadilkar**: refining the chapters and helping me add more depth
- **Dr. Mark Goulston** for the Foreword
- **Mr Rangaswami, Ian Woodley, Ian Gotts, Rana Olk, Omkar Nisal, Satish Shenoy, David Lee Jensen, Ken**

McArthur, Dr. Jeffrey Sampler, Naveen Lakkur:and Steve Sponseller for the advance praise

- **Sujatha Reghunathan, Kishor Venkatesh Rajeeva, Veeresha Hogesoppinavar, and the Verbinden Communication team**: for editing, and choosing and preparing the appropriate Napkinsights to go with the chapters

- **Rachel Voyles, Chris Shempra, Joe Polish** and **Dino Watt** for their permission to share their stories.

- **Rakesh Kakkar, Taruun R. Jha** and **Henrietta C Devine** for coming together to make an awesome promo video

- **Rohit Bhargava and team at Ideapress Publishing**: for getting this book out in record time

- **Parsifal and team** at Netherlands: for helping me with the marketing campaign for the book

- **Mike Martin** for early feedback on the book

- **Srini Gurrapu** for detailed feedback to tighten the chapters

- **Joshua Rozario** and team at Mindshare Digital: for the web presence for the book

- **Himanshu Khanna** and team: for the help with several design elements

- **Kshitij Minglani** for suggesting to add the "How to make the most out of this book" section

- **Manuj Aggarwal**: for feedback and help with the copy

- **Akshay Cherian** and team at MyBizSherpa: for collaborating on the reflection questions and more

- **Satish Shenoy** for valuable and specific feedback to make this a better book
- **Venkk Sastry** for detailed feedback chapter by chapter
- **Utpal Vaishnav** for detailed review of the early draft of the book
- **Guru Yellapur** for reviewing the late draft of the book
- **Mita Kapur** and team for their brilliant inputs on making this book better.
- **DP Sridhar** and **Naveen Lakkur** for collaborating on developing a few topics for the book

Lastly, my family, **Kavitha** and **Sumukh** for supporting all my ideas, even the crazy ones.

Rajesh Setty
Silicon Valley, April 2020

ABOUT RAJESH SETTY

Rajesh Setty is an entrepreneur, author, and teacher based in Silicon Valley. His latest startup is called Audvisor (www.audvisor. com) which features several thousand original micro-podcasts from world-class experts available at the push of a button. He has co-founded several other technology startups such as MentorCloud and Jifflenow.

Rajesh has written and published sixteen books so far with his first book published at the age of 13. Over the last few years, he has shared over 2,400 Napkinsights (www.napkinsights.com) and several of them have been featured on the first two volumes of ThinkBooks (www.gothinkbook.com).

Rajesh is an award-winning teacher at the Founder Institute where he has helped over 1,000 first-time entrepreneurs to bring their ideas to life.

LOOKING TO LEARN MORE?

If you have come this far, I already know that you are serious about upgrading yourself. Over a dozen insights from this book are packaged into short audio insights and made available via our app Audvisor. With Audvisor, you have access to several thousand micro-podcasts from over hundred world-class experts on topics of personal and professional development at the push of a button, wherever you are, whenever you want.

You can learn more about Audvisor here:
www.audvisor.com

9 781646 870257